MANSCAPE IN THE SIERRA

NEW & COLLECTED POEMS 1991-2011

Gbanabom Hallowell

Sierra Leonean Writers Series

Manscape in the Sierra
New and Collected Poems 1991 - 2011

ISBN: 978-99910-54-52-0

Sierra Leonean Writers Series

To my Dad, John

CONTENTS

Introduction by Yulisa Amadu Maddy

MANSCAPE IN THE SIERRA

Come Away My Love
Slides on the Ankle of Africa
Manscape in the Sierra
The Pus of the Sun
Dance Ebony
Trapped
Us
Camwood & Other Trees
Sierra Leone I Celebrate You
Threshold
Avril
Black Bone
Light
Lacuna
My Savannah Lover
English
I Go Under My Sweat
Flower Against the Wind
All I Know about All I Knew
Green, White & Blue
Truth & Reconciliation Commission
46664
After the Sun Had Gone Down

DRUMBEATS OF WAR

Drumbeats of War
Freetown, Freetown
Such Morning Roads
Night Shadows
The Dining Table
The Drawing Board
I've Never known that in the Land of the Dead
       Children Are Born though
       I know Dead People Idle in Bed
Fraudster
Offshoot
Elegy
Wall
Sleeves
Solitude After War
Hills of Temper
Philosophy & Water
Rejuvenate Me
Reigning in Blood
Let Me Speak for Myself
Our Developed Men
Roethke Writes
Ordinary Man
Preacher
I Climb the Height of Day
Milton Margai Teachers College
My Eyes are No Mirror
And These Shall Be the Signs
To say the Least

To a Broken Omolankay

I sing of Men I Pity

Countrypeople

She Carries it on Her Head Sideways

Rupture

In His Memory

Let Us Make a Yellow Joke

Threading the Void

Waterfronts

In the Deep Recesses of Hunger

We No Longer Write Poems in Camera

Portrait

Harmattan

Poet Unwanted

A Long Walk Home

Harvest

When the Clouds Become Too Thick

Great Scarcies, Little Scarcies

Of Windows and Shadows

On Their Blindness

The Diary of Pedro Da Cintra

Child Chooses His Path

The Sierra Leone I Love

Give Me Free!

A New Planet

Letter to My Dad

Late Last Night

Oblation

Everyman A Journey

In the Middle of My Journey, I Pause

Windows Are a Private Thing

Singing As a Poet

Trial

Venom

Memories of Home While Home in Exile

On Being Asked to Write a Poem for My Country

The Songs of Sia Leona

MY IMMIGRANT BLOOD

Strange Fruit

My Responsibilities As a People's Poet

Confluence of Hands

The Desert Speaks of Body Bags

The Long Walk to Motherland

The Cotton Tree Cries of Thirst

I Dream of Africa

My Sister, Thara

Along This Avenue Where I Live

The Middle Passage

O Mother

The Business of War

Night in Golgotha

Diary of an Imprisoned Journalist

The Chain

Trap

After This Vituperation

My Autobiography in Fifty Lines

My Immigrant Blood

Natural Selection

I Love the Breasts of Wangari Maathai

The Brutal Discovery

Drinking From the Cup of Life
Legacy of the Damned
The Million Man March
Night of My Wrath
Touch Me Every So Often
I Saw the Sky Catch Fire
I'm Walking on a Fine Bridge Across to Lungi
The Place Where People Dance No More
Of Exile and Certain Things
And of Exile and Certain Things
Again of Exile and Certain Things
Yet of Exile and Certain Things
The Permanence of Pain
The Beating of Bones

Gbanabom Hallowell

INTRODUCTION

It was with trepidation that I took on this daunting task to write an observation normally styled as an introduction to this volume of poems by Gbanabom Hallowell. I have never and will never again be so foolish to try again, even if it means losing a very close friend of kindred spirit.

Whatever my observations are and what I have written, I hope it is an introduction, a sharing with the reader; an insight on the troubled mind of the poet who in his own commitment and dedication reaches out and tells it as it is. In Mammy language, "*Leh we tawk am fine.*"

I am aware that I have not come anywhere near the poet's poems' original inner eye(s) searching—the lone restless spirit. Perhaps a poet and not a playwright/novelist could have done a better job, I don't know. But I do know that Gbanabom Hallowell's poems are not easy to comprehend. Their very simplicity makes them difficult. The economy of words, phrases and images, although impressive and mind provoking, forces one to take a long pause and begin to ask, who is Gbanabom Hallowell the man, the journalist, the poet?

Across the mirror of time the writer experiences many things that sustain him. Consequently and unconsciously, the poet stops and takes a searching look at what is on the other side of the mirror, stops and takes a look and wonder what drives the people, the men and women to distort their appearances, the family structure, the native language, and the very way they think and show love, affection and compassion for each other.

1

These examinations have a variety of names: the Atlantic slave trade, imperial colonialism, independence, neo-colonialism, economic enslavement, etc. We as a people, African people, Sierra Leoneans, have the tendency to always lapse out of these cycles into the same kind of degenerative, mimicking existence, only to lapse back into the self-inspecting, self-exploring cycle as in *Manscape in the Sierra: New and collected Poems 1991-2011* by Gbanabom Hallowell. Where does the pattern end?

The pattern ends when young writers like Gbanabom Hallowell, Mohamed Gibril Sesay, Moses Kainwo, Musu Sandy, etc., etc, take a definite stand on their "Discoveries" of themselves and refuse to be less than what they are. Building on that self knowledge, discovering what they are, and what they must be in the future. Gbanabom has dug up the "Roots" of slavery, colonial and neo-colonial roots that has been buried in obscurity and deception, while at the same time nurturing the plant-children—that must branch out, giving life, truth and immortality to all Sierra Leoneans.

Roots and branches, a declaration of Sierra Leonean Africaness, a view from the inside. The *'igbah-le'*; an attempt to sustain the new found cycle; and most of all a merger of the young and old, the past and present, the real and the imagined real, the magic of words and the magic of pictures, symbols, images and metaphors. I will be remiss if I do not confess how much I have learnt *that* I have for a long time taken for granted. Gbanabom, I am grateful for the opportunity.

Prof. Yulisa Amadu Maddy   *University of Makeni*

Praises for Gbanabom Hallowell's poetry

"The spirit of search pervades the whole collection with recurring images of the poet looking through windows into vast expanses of landscape and seascape, into the Lion Mountains of his country, into its trees, listening to the sound of its rivers, its birds and its people. [Gbanabom Hallowell] is always conscious of his responsibility as a poet to his country."

--Eldred Durosimi Jones, *Editor, <u>Africa Literature Today</u> and author, <u>Othello's Countrymen</u>*

"Gbanabom Hallowell's poems are evocative incantations at their best, moving with an hypnotic rhythm that, as Robert Hass says, is itself a political act in that all rhythm moves us. The lines keep shifting, in his characteristic way, between the large and small, making each define the other. He explores subjects…that range from overtly political to the personal, oftentimes counterpointing one against another to create an emotionally powerful statement. A number of the poems deal with his mother but also mother earth in a mythic way: indeed, Hallowell might well be described as a poet of powerful national myths, often using them to get at political and personal issues. In brief these are sophisticated poems of considerable accomplishment. I think he is a poet we will hear a lot from in the future."

--Richard Jackson, PhD
author, <u>Unauthorized Autobiography: New and Selected Poems</u>

"…a powerful collection of poems. The effortless merger of public and private spaces, feelings, thoughts and lives, and the visceral evocation of "lived" lives and "living" selves is refreshing. [The poet] branches an aesthetic consciousness that is innovative in both the syncretistic blend of traditional, personalized and allusive poetic imagery and a strong individual poetic vision couched in "social eyes".

-- Patrick K. Muana, Ph.D
Department of English, Texas A&M University

"Manscape in the Sierra: New and Collected Poems 1991-2011 by Gbanabom Hallowell, makes a broad sweep in diverse voices to sustain a single lamentation for the rescue of humanity. Africa, the continent of Eden, sent forth the people "in chains and chainless" to cultivate the earth, to mate and multiply; and from Africa comes voices whose echoes reach the four corners of the earth, whimpering of wars and rumors of wars, famine and diseases, and physical and mental destruction. Whatever the grand designs of scribes, chroniclers, prophets, peacemakers, or fools, world culture issues an architecture of skeletal remains, a valley of dry bones where one stands at "…the crossroads of…pregnancies…" that are empty promises of rebirth.

The poet pulls us into his universe to tell a very long story. The more we grow comfortable among the literary accessories, the more we note the poet's play on time and space, especially of the last three hundred years of human history. However, the history is not linear or circular. Rather, the markers are memory, spontaneous shifts in

4

consciousness, myths (ancient and contemporary), theories of evolution and identity formation. So, the universe Hallowell creates in the poems is being composed by way of a certain random-ness, each act of which contains the DNA of all other acts of random-ness. Similarly, reference to humanity in the "manscape" is singular and plural (one man/all men), even as Hallowell careens shyly around the cultural fixity of genders, his "voices" search for the new lexicon, the new grammar and the new linguistics, through which to extricate humanity from a prison-house of misnomers."

Fredrick Woodard, PhD
Poet and Emeritus Prof. of English, The University of Iowa

"Hallowell enlists his virile and visceral voice in the strident denunciation of a feckless and decadent national bourgeoisie that has wasted his nation's patrimony through an avoidable sanguinary harvest of blood. Through the deft deployment of images, dexterous manipulation of tropes, accomplished mobilization of martial metaphors, the creative husbandry of language with its sign systems, he moulds a poetic universe that is simultaneously down-to-earth, powerful and compelling."

--James Tar Tsaaior, PhD
Centre for General Studies, Lagos State University, Ojo, Nigeria

"When he is writing at his best, Gbanabom Hallowell combines the nomenclature of classic surrealism with a vivid and evocative portrait of his native culture, he also writes poignantly about the consequences of political upheaval and exile."

--David Wojahn
Award winning poet and author of <u>Strange Good Fortune</u>

"The pages of this collection are splashed with potent imagery; alliteration impregnates assonance, giving birth to syllables of dreams and memories. Sexual imagery abounds in the book; and it is a fitting imagery as it embodies a vision of the birth of a new "human condition" devoid of sterility and aridity. In other words, the oasis must replace the desert, "public-ease" the "secretpain," so that Sierra Leone, and for that matter, the world, may not be 'overrun by carbon dioxide.'"

--Sheikh Umar Kamara, Ph.D
Department of Languages & Linguistics, Virginia State University

"Gbanabom Hallowell is a poet worth waiting for in future!"

--Syl Cheney-Coker,
author, <u>The Graveyard Also Has Teeth</u> and <u>Sacred River</u>

MANSCAPE IN THE SIERRA

COME AWAY MY LOVE

Come away my love.
Go through the nine pence of the hour.
I love you ambidextrously; and even with the power
of my left hand alone I sing you these songs
from the soul of the Sierra after
the sparrows had flown away.

SLIDES ON THE ANKLE OF AFRICA

To the extent that the lion veil slides on the ankle
of Africa, artists return, over and over
on this road to figure out the furnace of the Sierra.
Starlight of the horizon mapping the edges
of the continent, *Span-yard* of the African Sierra,
open on the inside as much as on the outside.
Your identity lies on the breath of history
against the door distancing itself in your watery presence.
Brother of the Madre, your Spain and your Portugal
ascend the tropic temper of the African ranges.

Theories of water, the bellicose sea
acts against its own Rokel, against its dissatisfied
waves, knowing too well that the sovereignty of Europe
is still active within the belly of the African peninsula.
O sea, haven't you also consumed the food of Songhai
or wasted along the Gold Coast to sip a drink?
Where is the eye with which you saw the lion
when it was possessing the mind of the continent?
Suggest to me the left foot of your thought, and
I will condemn myself to be your poet!

MANSCAPE IN THE SIERRA

At once the war returned to its abode, the bellies
of its owners, to die-awake. Consoling the hour
the wind of God came through the nostrils
of our understanding and we were separated
from the dead: a river of two corpses with their
lugubrious access to the deep sea, dead bones
in water to water dead bones; alluvial corpses
and their revolvers of tired smoke gathered their harvest,
broke their guns to make them flutes. All the dead
woke and with one blow fell the Cotton Tree.

Pergola supporting pergola upon two urchins
and a mother inhaling her breath with which she
had disowned her fruits. The harvest became a destiny
and the road a destiny; the journey a destiny, and
the moment a destiny; sorrow the destiny of sadness
and joy the destiny of madness. War the destiny
of war and also the destiny of peace. In the end
the soldier became the weeping civilian with a father
and a mother to bury and with a son to narrate his life to;
a daughter to offer to the man whose wife he shot in the back.

An aftermath of confluence: the tributaries at the edge
of the river's conscience; the road with a million urgent

steps wrapped around the reluctant mountain and a
    discretionary
peninsula; the drums and the croon incapable of separating
cries from laughter; an automobile of young minds
drove their spirits into shrines with a global viper; a market
stall where ragged men exchanged guns for love; the wearied
hours surged with spontaneity and gathered besides
the evening heath, besides those who could only talk about
heroes and thought of them as gods. There, the hours waited.

Yesterday the last sniper was silenced and his gun stolen.
A blatant morning walked into town with a placard in hand
returning Freetown to Freetown. Who will take a drenched
city by the hand? How does one account for a shift in Pedro's
gaze? Where did the lion lay his mane when the city
dropped from the grips of a child who had lost a limb, a life,
sitting on a riffle and not a machete? A revolutionary
clogging waterways so they no longer gather as rivers
or the hills as mountains. Where were the gates
of Athens erected when that European city was founded
on these African plains? In the end, the city dropped
from the grips of a child who himself had lost a limb and a life
sitting on a rifle and a machete left behind by a revolutionary.
The waterways no longer gathered as rivers, or the hills as
mountains.

In the aftermath of the war, a silent silence moved around
the Sierra, taking the country under its wings. Ten thousand
birds flew in to occupy the country's airspace with rifles of figs.
Let the undertaker forget his trade and become a carpenter;
let the rescue team be turned into fishermen and let them
set out in the small hours. Let the day pass into the diaphane
of the night and the night into the heart of the day .
A tsunami of bricks of that bloody decade has collapsed in the
 sea—the sanctimonious pyramids of war and all that was in it
have sunk into the reddened sea of a desolate Egypt.

THE PUS OF THE SUN

And every time a sweat drops off a leaf
I hiccup like a troubled heart. The history
I was born into noted that my race
came directly from the sun.

I come along to you like coffee
but it is up to you to determine things
like cream, sugar or honey drop
and remember, that is not a thought but a fact.

The time has come again for another sweat to drop
off a leaf. There is a god in that lone sweat; no wonder
my black is gold.

The rays of the sun are now heavier than
those of the winds touching my body
with the wet nose of a dog
and the appetite of a road.

There is no longer the fur of anger
I thought it had and my eyes
no longer run with tears of fear.
There are more people living in the sun
than are there on earth sweating
the leaves of trees.

Between sweats I tender my love to the leaves
and between leaves my love suffers under sweats
the green of death ignites
a corollary of genital passion.

Rays of passion, doors of angels
on accidental plateaus.
The quick thrall of affairs of conjugal
birds scraping the backs of the skies
before the descent
to become me in favor of my race.

Contemplating the sweat because of the leaf
and the leaf because of the sweat
and my eyes from which a smoke, bearing
a diagram look deeply at a thought
designed to be an un-thought.

A total eclipse of leaves has wiped
off the brow of the sun and I no longer
expect men from my race to come forth
in less evolutionary fashion. My son shall
emerge with an exclamation and only
our similar god-mark shall speed our bond.
It is only because of this promise
that I still look into the eyes of the sun—
the god of my race.

DANCE EBONY

Color is elegance in dancing;
So the whole of this lyric can only be of ebony

about the gyrating moments running off my grips
into desert telephones, heel-deep sand dune.

Night is on collision with me in this desert
and it feels good if cold water should run over my feet.

The calmness of the oases is in the best of intentions
and at the moment a dozen squirrels are snorting
my rattling feet.

TRAPPED

Like an angel in long-tale wings
I dare the nuclear gardens
where you and I were separated
from each other centuries ago
when the world knew not any naked mortal.

I see white wings in your beer
gulped over your macabre
laughter; and tonight I should
have been long gone but the road
has not yet returned.

Therefore shall I ask
for an apple and quicken my loincloth?
I don't know, I don't know
I don't know how to be Ham's son
without the loincloth
of our two self-same;
and remember, night must not fall
on us both in this forbidden place.

US

Between us two the river runs deep;
between the eyes of the fingers that don't move;
between the color of our minds the waters turn salty;
between us a stone has taken life and gone
out of our existence.

what is the meaning of a colorless water
wrapping around my black bone?
Who wears a shoe to go on a journey?
Why are there too many questions in my bag
instead of adhering to the Bethlehem advice
of the Christ who himself lost
an experience and a shoe on the road to Capernaum?

Between us a window has chosen to be rude.
Brother, only our sweats can silence this window
and turn away the birds about to perch on its sill.

The fact is that we have forgotten about the war
and left all its memory in the brains of the dead;
so, what does it matter to us that this Eden
rains in blood? Haven't we surrendered our hearts
to this miserable place and renamed it the Eden of Den
so that the centuries we know would not
be the centuries our children should know?

I am going away from myself and so must you
and for this singular action a ruined road
could be rebuilt.

CAMWOOD AND OTHER TREES

Forest, I am going to feed you my body
when I die, so that you will grow
into a giant the constipation of my name.
It took me just this lifetime
to will myself to you.
Even my roots are yours. My will to you is a bird
flying into many eyes.

If I die on a rainy day
allow your leaves to shake
their egos over my carcass
so that the trees themselves
shall beckon to me
Gbanabom Gbanabom Gbanabom

The mortal mouth cannot pronounce my name, because
the font of human linguistics is only full of hosannas
of hosannas of hosannas of voiceless bilabial plosives.

Haven't I died already?

SIERRA LEONE I CELEBRATE YOU

Then shalt thou cause the trumpet of the jubilee
to sound…in the day of atonement shall ye make
the trumpet sound throughout all your land.

Leviticus Chapter 25 v 9

Sierra Leone I celebrate you!
I celebrate your persistent love and your careful anger
Africa's fandango dance shall put a crown on your head
I celebrate your temper and your soul
Because of you the cerebral moment explodes in me
Even as your fences bend backwards and inwards
The vagabond is able to breathe a sigh of relief
So I celebrate your oases and their fervor
I celebrate your two hands that pick the yoke off my head
And your two minds that walk along the main avenue in town
Front to front and back to back
Searching out the urchins and the places that harbor them
I celebrate your lugubrious years
Because of which you have grown to be 50
I celebrate your rivers and your mountains
And your history buried in their bellies
I celebrate you in contemplation
Of the past the present and the future
Veritable country I celebrate the lion that is in you

The lion that rests its mane on the waters of the aged
I celebrate your bones and the patient flesh that covers their
        backs.
I celebrate your agony because your agony itself celebrates you
Agony is fertile in your womb O country of the amphibian
But so is your passion, so is your passion of the while
I celebrate your desperate love and your desperate heart

Though your tribal marks have dented your looks
I celebrate your ubiquitous desire
To be a mother and a daughter too
Look at your footprints on the sands of time
And the calmness of the landscape under them
When I think about the wilderness shoved into your throat
And the cancerous desire of the slave driver to put you down
I tremble with joy at the patience of your authentic hurricane

        --They crushed the dove in your hands
        --They crushed the snail of your legs
        --They crushed the viper of your eyes
        --They crushed the butterfly of your mind

Yet unable to humble the lion that you are
Therefore I celebrate your Christianity and your Islam
The two parts of your mind that have accepted your perfidious
Children who for a long decade served you blades to eat

Your Wara Wara is on my mind
And so are your Great and Little Scarcies
I emerged from the cracks
When the Aberdeen broke its creek
O Bunce, you dragged an Island into my soul
Through the garrisoned tightness of my Freetown

In all of these you held yourself breasts to breasts
As we your children smelled your armpits of love
Mama Salone, I salute your motherhood!

THRESHOLD

O road, walk me gently through my golden jubilee
Fifty waters on my cobra conscience
I taste of vinegar on the back of ancient leaves
My mind was sane when my sole took to you
Forsaking all others heel-to-hill under grey stones
In taking you, the other roads demise in me

Road to road the mind is oblivious of the footprints
When yesterday merges with tomorrow
Memory takes the form of water and
The shape of a river is achieved
Road, always remember me as a valley
A threshold in the emptiness of years
So that when I wriggle in time
My days come back to me as water and river

Today my sole makes a pact with you
Do not give me away to the shadows
And I will balance my weight on you accordingly
Between you and I no journey exists
Because you traverse the currents of time
In the very same way that I traverse frequency
I have left behind me a symposium of birds
Singing of a golden jubilee inside of which

Existed several decades of iron-bars
And only you could have helped me go through
Those decades like water in the mind of a river
Road, only you can tell me what else
Could be found inside the belly of a golden jubilee
A golden Jubilee has no belly, did I hear you say that
The bottom of a jubilee may look like a belly
But it is actually an endeavor to look pass the self

Therefore, today I deny myself a bench
Leaving it behind, I shall dare the threshold
O road, I am left handed just as I am right handed
Never mind the intellectual mist in the middle of a myth
My left hand is just as friendly as my right hand is
Utterly Sierra Leonean, I linger in fourteen minds
Wishing to forget all the wretched stories I know
But how can I be too sure about which stories to keep
When I am still tangled in that ancient tower

And in spite of my verrucas my journey sweetens
On your terra-cotta back sangfroid in your vestibule
It is good to turn fifty in your company
Where a dolorous past can suffer abatement
Already the moon has spat another day in my face

And tonight the *boubou geng*[1] will approach me

With their metaphysics to seek the simplicity in me
That philosophers, have been blind to for fifty years
If I were to ask for a birthday gift it would be
The heart of the lion Pedro ran off with to Portugal
And the excavation of Athens from my blood

---

[1] *Boubou geng: cultural festival*

AVRIL

O moon,
eater of the gender cake
Sweeten your mouth
with Avril's golden jubilee
Brought forth on the Savannah of an African dawn
That anxious hour when the undertaker
became a father, the barren master
beat his head into ploughshares

Plovers of the Queen,
the African mollusc, hardened
by your beak, no longer touch soft, no longer touch soft
House of Lancaster, you remember very
well the Molotov cocktail for HRM
The eve Avril turned twenty-seven
times in her mother's belly
Mixing with the stentorian voices
of the Sierra and of the Rokel
That night the horizontal fathers grabbed
their hoes and took off, returning
with the herbal resolve
to replace the plovers of the Queen

Colonial apertures of the burrow
Avril no longer wants to hold her hand tight to a paper skin

Even if you come *fak-am bec gbasi-am bec*[2]
With your fierce and blind train of nocturnal conscience
The rain shall burrow into your garrisoned tracks

Avril,
erect your palisade in the temper of men
After the celebrations
have passed over into shadows
Between two dreams
that know of your palatine desire
Whether they speak of a world
that tomorrow would bring in envelopes
Or of the embers of untold stories
written in hard rocks
In the end, it is your celestial vision
that keeps the vermin in their places
Therefore, like the stone
fifty years only goes through your veins
Like the normal blood;
somewhere inside of you remains a larva
That never adjourns—

---

[2] *fak-am bec gbasi-am bec: Themne expression of the cacophonous sound of a passing train; also serving as a metaphor of endless servitude*

BLACK BONE

I

Born in the imagination of the man
who cracked his own egg
spewed his inscrutable sperm
I am October the truly tropical layer
of the ozone over the Atlantic
I am November, the soul of the savannah
A collarbone running through the diaphragm
of space with all kinds of longitudinal attitudes

I was born where the world is most nervous
where pregnancy is never taken
where prose is slave to verse
and Dante accounted as yet another master

I was born in the Rokel River
where the clouds
stood on the back of a universal crocodile
to throw a javelin
to the compromising center of the earth
The rural poet wrote my birth in fevered ink

II

Actually I'm not yet born
I await the Januaries
in the laager for the festival of being

The earth stands between
my conception and my birth
because the earth must first
register me before I proceed

My birth like everyone else's is an imagination
while I grow in the concept I shall
not grow in my birth
I shall have reached the rock of being
touching its tip as the sea touches shore
O earth! server of the chalice
mouth of the asclepiadaceous wine
O earth, make me not your earthling

I am horseshoe of the desert
camel of the oases
I do not wish to walk the earth
clinging to a name
do not wish to be associated
with the earth's dust

I have a sandal in my chest to
remember always my arrival
at some place where the earth is not

known as a planet
I am rain of time fading on two-edged places
The heavens flush me; the earth also flushes me

III

Listener, let me take you into my bosom
like the ocean does with giant mammals
who do not fit in riverbed seas
that you can see the wider paths
of the narrow lanes you see in my palms
There are trees and there are rocks
actually, the inside of me
is no different from the outside
but when you come into me
you are certainly going to return

fully informed about my scatological being
In me is a disaster of tapeworms
but do not take them for granted
They lie quietly on the pale
substance of my intestines

IV

At the third hour of every living day
I orchestrate my thinking
passing under the rough bridge
of the dead, waiting for someone to soothe my skin
I have to be careful not to celebrate
the breath of life
I have stolen from the caged
as I know full well that the gods have run
short of the raw materials
used to create men who leap into unexpected months
without their own mothers having broken their waters
My desire is to recreate myself
to make of myself
at least a mortal god
and descend in spirit form like a kite of clouds
detaching a part of me
from the larger firmament of my sciosophy
the palatine longing of a restless bird
I fly without perching
reaching to the west wind
the east wind, ducking to embrace
the south wind and the north wind also
The four edges of the cardinal
paralyze between the fingers of my skills

31

my left hand grading the geography
of Semo Sancus

V

I attended mass this morning
To have someone sooth my skin
There I encountered the woman
in the middle of the storm
I did not pray to have her
content with my own Adam

She came anyway!
lying to me
that a god had pushed her off a cliff
on flight-fall
the imbalance of airplane
whose shaking wings
capsize on my
diminutive forest of thorn-
bordered purgatory
Dante breathed his last
into her magical stone
pulling from her the lodged pole
of the gods in her throat

The bullets in her eyes
are already done
another garden has lowered
with its own apple tree

That morning the rain changed its mind
no longer beating like a drummer
because of this new woman walking
away with the rib
stuck in her rattling hair
She is crying for a man not among
those she bedded
Tomorrow is anxious in her eyes
where a snake is playing a flute
in all her prowess she keeps crying about
an hour
a small key
locked behind the teeth of
a crowded Jerusalem
Her morning is an open barn
full of lazy feathers
I am not standing on her way—
this approximate woman!
Wherever she goes in the garden
she leaves a breast behind
What manner of man can boast of catching

up with this kind of revolution
when to expose the gods
the woman invites the man to attend
to her geography
whose contours promise to open eyes
with warm water from revolvers

VI

I am familiar with that ancient fear—
the fear of doors!
The single door being the impossible kind
I have to let you know this urgent matter before
the rib cuts into your skin
Eve is armed this time around! Quick enough
to snatch from the palm of the gods
She walks the desert and sails the sea
with man's most essential organ

VII

Pass an eye on me like a razor
I am he whose flesh is soft
make a festival for my blood
and I shall dance with my toes on fire
Imagine my name, but don't pronounce it

34

spell it on the leaf of a dagger
don't mourn because you slit my throat
You'd have conquered death in her finest hour!

VIII

The beloved garden broke a new soil last night
I see its boarders pegged on the rock
on which the two breasts of the only Lucifer laid

The land and the chrome are dark
I am the beggar eyes of the comets
with the hunger the temptation
intended to nibble
Into my intestines; and so today
I prepare for the serpent's
final Passover which shall be marked
with the spider's scatological trap

"Descend from your colony of sky
and posses the garden of life!"

Feudal engine, the mechanics
have lost their battles

the dietetics no longer reading
the same in their minds—
sputter the devil on the cross

IX

Because of you I have this anthropological wound
The chalice of my ageless agony—
but I shall no longer detain
a child within. I bring her forth dipolar of my science
against your diocese—
this tinted chip

I coax the sun in my hand
to use as a weapon against your image
your tires have crushed my wares
in more than one lifetime
and now we meet on the only path
one lifetime one path and you must reinvent yourself
O conquered dinosaur—
coaxing another ice age in your heart

X

And I shall sing an ode to Eve, the rainmaid
Before now she brought the rain, and the

sunservant too brought the rain
before now the garden always wiped a brow
and the ocean always drank some more

But when the choral throat of this mammal went dry
sand-dune desert of mind dragged a famished ego
between equal clock time
kith and kin oases of the broken
a birth of ocean dances—
no need rain no need to palter
cloudward, O water of air
running the bottom of sky
no mane no name

When two jaws can no longer whiten the molars
we say the tongue has lost its taste
and when the gum suffers a cowardly lick
wisdom is missing from the mouth
a yawn slips in with a breath—
germ of drawl
germ, octave upon octave
piano knocking notes
the sky of hope knocks down a dove
and the hunter picks up a vulture
a diner instead of a dinner
an accident has occurred!

LIGHT

Kiss earth O hands on ground
soil's paraphernalia on the inevitable brother-
a humility leaving a dozen pain in posterior heads
between ablutions of no organized *kaaba*
and scattered beads itching aged toes owl and prowl
night never being a nectar on the bloodless taste
I rise unto my waist towel-stripped tongue
And this memory of the oasis when it was full
itched the back of the desert the desert of the back
speaking of back I'm devoid of metaphors
but of dried eyes dripping of blood
in my Sierra trapped in the legend of the dark!

My official hunger defined me on morning roads
avoided even by procrastinating bats
I have crushed into imaginary trees
no longer fit to serve the name of the forests
all my days were irrelevant to me
walking on Painful Street in the middle of town
The *waleng*³ came mid-day in malarial simplicity
turning yellow the eyes of the night owl
the scandalous road danced in my eyes
but I already knew the crossroads of such pregnancies
and this time when this new child is born
its sole shall not be limited to soils of the Black Lane!

---

³ *Waleng: Themne word for Light*

38

LACUNA

Confidence in the eyeglass, not in the eye
in the staircase, never in the stairstep;
in the wing, not in the bird
and in yourself alone, in yourself alone, in yourself alone.
Cesar Vallejo

Half of me is on the road
while the other half contemplates
hanging itself on a tree.
The distance between the two is philosophical:
the one half man wears a ring on
the right thumb of the left hand;
the other half man wears
a chain backward around the neck

A viper crosses my heart
meeting with the black bone of my vinegar
I have a versatile feeling this morning
that tonight will come upon
my head variously unprepared
for the spices in my wounded bodices.

Be it as it may, all will be well with the lone
thought on the lone road of Petrovsky lacuna.
Listen to me hard because the walls

have gone deaf on this spot where I stand;
listen to the archaeological rotation of the day
and to the beggar who insists on helping
your course with a lone penny;
and to the urchin whose poverty is rich with life.
In this Sierra the poor have confidence in their poverty
while the rich always swim to some place to drown.

My two self-same dine on the caustic
annotation of the road that separates me;
of the tree always ready to hang;
of the joyous women absent in my death; and
of the perimeter knowledge turning un-knowledge.

This morning the media came right at my head
calling me all kinds of names.
There was the *Independent Observer* which
like any *Dependent Observer* and other prints
lied to my dead mother that they couldn't
reach my mouth. They assumed I was already dead.

The journalists and I are both
writing in different rooms
during the battle we couldn't
give a name to; this poem shall live longer
to correct the ink of the press.

I saw a gun in one newspaper this morning
with fingerprints traced to me but with
an editorial in denial of my involvement
as the corpse vanished in space.
Beware O Sierra! I am that corpse!

MY SAVANNAH LOVER

Not after that hour when you and I had agreed
here in this grassland that a cat has walked
into our lives defining our conjugal desire—

that the distant trees shall create a clearing
for us to spread our tablets against
an imaginary Sinai;

not for the absence of the bread shall we
lose a hold of the gown of night
and the effervescence of the animal river.

Rachael, daughter of Rachael
you know all too well what wind shall
blow against this grassland
before the morrow
evolves in the throat of the past.

I claim my gloves on your hands,
come closer without an apostrophe
and I shall look upon you
with a provincial desire. Glove of my glove,
hand of my hand follow me
to the fire where the furnace glows.

Because of you I dream of crosses against
which I have wrestled Cupid, and for this act
I hope to remove the chaos in your eyes.

If I swirl in your territorial heart
then come away from the smoke
of your broken house,
together we can lower the height
of this peninsular hill.

My soul has arrived from a lugubrious mansion,
Godspeed, reversing seven years in Laban's labor
wanting, only, to reside where the grass is green
far from the weak eyes in desolate places.

Follow me to the branches
where these precise birds perch;
in spite of ourselves let us
seek the green towel in the immediate
trees and rinse our two souls
as one life in the beaks of the singing
birds of this lonely Savannah.
We shall celebrate our preciseness
in theirs so that when they come
to trust our shadows their plumages
shall shelter the body of our density.

ENGLISH

This language before which I fall on my knees
owes me an apology. This language
with its shipwrecked grammar and impossible
linguistics has second-rated my frustration.

Knowledge of good and evil I have a false tree
planted in my desert after my Rokel
was murdered in its basins. Tell the English Queen
that my sorrows are not in her words
but in their meanings.

English alacrity steps too lightly
on my tropical concerns
puffing off all its winter ego
in my father's barn. I can
go to war every minute to lay my hand of hope
on my father's corpse or his dutiful remains
for I know how much of it has died and
how much remains alive.

Language of my garrison your slave is always
going and coming back, always
full of your vocabularies,
always rummaging your useless books. You make

my mother smile in her corpse,
believing that I can bury her
with the sentiments of your bitter colony.

Accent of the royal speed mind the primitive consciences
of these conquered plateaus; their lonely tributaries
run the blood of thirst sowed by your feat of navigation.

This promiscuous tongue of mine is sore from its many flutes
the quadriplegia of the faithful revolver shooting at my tropics.

I have uttered many boastful statements in English
which I cannot replicate in my mother tongue.
I know now that you are not a mother but a step-mother.
Many a poet have questioned
their black Anglo-Saxon against your snow.
I am questioning your intention as you ride on a broom
over my continent, my African continent silencing
its agricultural languages.

Where is your soul O English?
After being condemned to read in you I do not cry
I do not know how to console my mother tongue;
do not know how to assure her that I am forever
close to her, to her calabash of mind; do not know
how to make conversation without being bookish;

do not know how to control my stammer
when crossing the river of your super Grammar
to come back home and lie on the lap of my mother.

English, you are now the language of my thirst;
therefore, I too seek to imprison you,
to teach you how to listen to the tongue of my mother,
to teach you how to quietly ride on your broom
over the musings of my grand-mother's
thousand tongues and to make you
citizen of this Babel.

I GO UNDER MY SWEAT

I go under my sweat,
under its phallic temper; the gecko goes
under its sweat, under its beastly nostrils;
the fire goes under its furnace
under its hell of purification.
The furnace returns to its sun,
made blind by its own destiny.

The republic is not yet so lucky;
therefore, it only has its armpit to go under;
the tongue goes under itself, wrapping
around the largess of its own Samaritan.

My lover goes under me with a fierce distrust
as I go under my moral fly—
The poet goes under his verses, under
the rejected manuscript because
conformity goes under the skin of creativity.

All I know today is about the things that surged;
the ferry that poked its dog nose in the territory
of the seabird. The airplane that crashed
under the unexpected snow in Antananarivo for love.

The wind that stopped breathing for miracles;
the child that spoke in its mother's womb;
the kettle that consumed the fire. In all of these,
my hand carried my soul, sipping the magic.

It is in the news that finally the Sierra Leone
war will go under a red hand—the end will then
begin to emerge at the beginning with an apex
very much like that of the Freetown cotton tree.
It is established that the war will only tell
of fruits: the mango, scattered all over like guns,
the orange, the pawpaw and the guava until
all that is committed to memory will be only juice.

The famous republic lies
under the sun,
contemplating sadness
in handkerchief,
contemplating metaphors
in finger count;
contemplating superstition
in threshold spot; contemplating me.

In all of these I am the factor
The country is allowed to trespass in my sorrow;
in the way I recollect the war. The country
is the sweat I go under.

FLOWER AGAINST THE WIND

To arrive at this point
it was necessary we had a deliberate history
tucked in the shame of our black bone
with the furnace of our ties
showing the incredible eyes of the cemetery mirror
that way the dead will look at the living and
the living at the dead
two corpses will walk up the road to talk about
the land of the living
about the betrayal of life
the cost of childhood
and the controversy will be on the trees
which hear all of these

trouble is brewing in the afternoon of my country:
the living and the dead are fighting over the phrase
'the son of the soil." To have arrived
at this point with the heads of state
rolling on the dust of the only path outside the city
rolling on their own blood
over and over again
rolling after the machete had spoken
rolling away before the next assignment
only because neither the mother nor the father
can determie who the son of the soil is

49

the yardstick is cleared by the forest stick
the handkerchief is on the sad end
and so is the black shoe usually common on the road
trinkets in the town square
trinkets in the home bottle
on the lives of these trinkets the country lost a decade
blur trinkets blur trinkets blur trinkets
lovers of gold will be lovers of gold
and to that truth is the concerns about dynamites
laid on the path of goers of the narrow end
the belle is adorned with trinkets
and so also is the drum-singer
but can they all by themselves tell
who the son of the soil is?

The duty bone is over chewed in the dog's mouth
as always in the dog's mouth
slave of the mortal monster
where is the answer? World of calcium
the duty bone is vanishing
the road and the journey remains unfinished
and the drought is sailing in
the river also has an interest in the duty bone
and for that it is washing itself up to land

ALL I KNOW ABOUT ALL I KNEW

Not including the headcount of the unknown
and the basket of chicken that flew over Saturn
or the incendiary whistle of the furnace of the sun
there is the body against the light of heaven
thrashed out of its human dreams, wrapped
around its own name, around its own occasion

Therefore, even the feeling of witness
could be said to be around that energy, and
a substantial effort of it appeared like a reluctant
broom seeking to devastate the jaws of history
by putting into all the remembered events
additional knives and machetes

Of those macabre catalogues, one, redder
than blood tortures the memory. A life
stripped of God and an invented image
defined the lot of the souls that passes through
this hot memory heading for the city library
to burn all the books with its raging silence

A chronicle of tributaries challenges the Rokel
swelling its belly with fire and archaeology. Can this
lot ever be forgotten? An infant squeezed out of its
voice, a mother forced to take her into pregnancy

51

belly-point. A larva of Medusa slips in with
the innocent and the ignorant—O Rokel

There is this one which can only go through
the fierce door of the human mind. Perpendicular
to the portrait of the perpetrator
in post-mortem. Up against a tenebrous dyslexia
the memory collapses in pain, and at once
a multiplicity of doors in colors and in signals

Then the rifles retreat behind emerging
green leaves, behind its own hot palms
with its palate licking the blood of victims, and
what sticks up memory was the quiet fear
creeping into the blade of the conscience
of the perpetrator of its own bumper harvest

Then the day that was already there came again
wide open with the boots of the Harmattan, bringing
its conscience to rest on the common skin; the
train moved along its tracks into oblivion, but
the somber hissing lived beyond the train, as
the chain of Sierra Leoneans replaced the surge

Finally, I know about the question in his face, and
the question in the face of the woman who died

under him; about the words that placed a gun
in his hands, and the reason he shivered under
his disagreeing self; about why he chose the long
bush path, and why he happily turned the gun on himself

GREEN, WHITE & BLUE

Always between the two of us
personal memories perish. Words
are mouthful of three
layers, and so warm
bread of solitude
goes between us with its unbaked flour
loincloth of the soldier
this body speaks of guarding
the Sierra, a life on a flying cloth
a phrase in the wind
the soul of a country in separatist fist
the man a soldier
the woman a soldier
the child a soldier
the-gone-beyond a soldier
all hanging on the cultivation
all hanging on the promise of tranquillity
all hanging on the muscles of the sea
centimetre by centimetre
you are a human flag
I roll on your colours against
the mind of your height
always flying high in the tree of my heart
squeezing between my fjord
and erecting your anthem

in the inside of me
because regardless
of the storm, I love you; and
your liberty is tested against
the east wind
where there is no west
the north wind
where there is no south
and yet you are my cardinal point
country of the extreme
waving welcome and waving goodbye
in your warm bread of solitude
so that before you I do not know
whether in coming I go
whether in going I come
I am the exiled child
with your bread in the hand
I am the Harmattan urchin passing through
ten doors of a decade and a decade of ten doors
I do not come to you in sirens
I know about your pre-decade torture
in the hands of sirens on boots
flying in the full blast of their lust

I come to you like a child
child of the reed-field
watching you wave
that bloody century back to the sea

TRUTH AND RECONCILIATION COMMISSION

With a bag of sorrows you came to the Sierra
as you say, to hunt for souls in the lone perimeter
of the lost world; you step into this macabre
desert by the door, collapsed in its own occasion.
A quiet wind passed you by on its way out,
and all you did was to ignore its body touch;
instead, you were fascinated by the dusty cobwebs
of silence in the broken room; that template
in your eyes was blind to the singers of the anthem.

In the Sierra, the rivers are interim, the mountain-tops
are interim, the veil is interim, the gathering
is interim, the truth is interim because the saints
are interim, scores of the past come in interim
gowns with the embers of the night before.
Even the mind is interim, incapable of reconciling
the burden of the algebraic war in Sierra terms.
The fireside is interim under the greedy pot,
under the greedy corpse whose sorrow you seek.

Wait, hey brother, hey sister commission a moment
to reconcile with your sandal, with the smoke
of your eyes before you embrace my Sierra.
Beware, there is too much Africa in local nodding;
beware of the vertigo in the membrane of the land;

57

beware of the martyrs in whose defence you sold
a pair of your shoes; beware of the hour you spend
in the company of the heroes, and of the distance
you set between you and the perpetrators, beware.

In the end it is not about what lizard would
fashion a revolver in the crowded room, but
about what the international reporter imagine
would sell if a lizard fashioned a revolver
in the crowded room; in the end it is not
about how the amputated waist would make love;
it is about how the international reporter
fashion the amputated waist would make love
in broken beds while the perpetrator looked on.

A Diaspora of repentance has turned into dust,
and the technical bones and their books are sunk
in a dry well of scarce phosphorus; the door
no longer opens outside but in the inside
where the passage has been crowded by those
who came to the discomfort of those who resided.
A chaotic jackal is in tumult in the middle; a brother
has disengaged from the fratricidal brother
over the virgin blood in the threshold of the door

46664

Between those numbers lies a patient bone
More silent than the deepest death

Between my eyes lies a follicle of hair
Longer than the Nile and the shadow of the Nile

Between the kindled embers of Africa
Lies the orb of an eye more single than a thought

In the intermingling of 10,000 dead men a soul rattles
And a subterranean resolve is achieved

The impossibility of Roben ties an island to days and nights
While the Sunday bible looks on in the eyes of the tired
masters

Between the sweats of the century and between the sweats
Of the black toes of prisoner-ship, the heartbeat is counted

The sanctimonious European walks pass the prison gates
With two cats under his armpits, with three signs under his
          nose

The rest of those in that community wear their colored
Clothes in the morning, at noon and in the evening

Toward the hour of memory the Sierra sheds its skin
And a country showers by the banks

Between the fists of these impossible numbers
Lies the dream of a stubborn fighter!

AFTER THE SUN HAD GONE DOWN

One day after the sun had gone down
over my head
my eyes looked at my chest
and took the bread from my left hand, gave it
to the right hand. This was not even during
the war in which it was customary for eyes
to favor the right hand over the left hand in the rough
affairs of mortality;
but even so, my soul in anger disengaged from my heart
leaving the chest a bare landscape of withered hairs.

The bread, gone from my left hand left me as left as ever
and I no longer was capable of accepting the right side
of my human right in the total jungle of animal right.
It was not the bread that was the bread
nor was it the chest that was the chest;
it was not the eye that was on high.
It was the fact that the war had gone
with all its baggage of why it was ever fought
it was because another moment
refused to emerge with its own children.

DRUMBEATS OF WAR

DRUMBEATS OF WAR

Rattling drumsticks bite dusty soles and
quicksteps like vibrating organs rise to measure
chord-worth— a final readiness to leave the planet
pulsating a million nameless silences and
breathless moments for the planet in which
 the hands of the clock stick into the red eyes
of the sun—leaping to equal the conga beats
of the *bata* of skin of the wild to the clitoridean
effects of rhythms and elements known to be sweet
 humming sounds inside the heads of gods—

FREETOWN, FREETOWN

Towards the end the wagons
derail and head for my dreams
shaking my entire body. Luckily
in my camwood silence the stream
of consciousness with its usual metal
surgery does not go through my hot
muscles; but I always experience
the barbed wired train rattling through
me with a saccharine treachery.

I am frustrated by my hypogeal screams
capable of echoing and sending sounds
into the rotten ears of restless corpses
known to belong to the tribe who dwell
in skyleaves and draw lines
in the belly of the skies, roaming
for blood over serpentine valleys
with the eternal thirst of Dracula;
and I shake in my sleep witnessing
the TV in the nocturnal eyes of birds
casting the troubled train with
immaculate pictures of shame
butchering—the sun dragging its tail
across the morning dampness to perch
on the desert branches with its camera—

waiting for the knock-kneed morning
flowered flames heating the armpits
of my country`s vultures—skyleaf dwellers
descending without flapping their
plumages to prey on yellow corpses.

Every time I dream of Freetown
my wind-dust spirals a penumbral
peninsula. I pulsate close-knit
leaf-like, running memory inside
my veins with the blood of my blood.

SUCH MORNING ROADS

Break between trees with rainbow
blood of men made from desert
stones that create imprints shaped on the back
of Harmattan leaves every time the monsoon
dances inside rainforest calabash.

The strange thing about rainbow blood is its taste
found on the lips of yellow leaves—a road
being a throat, war itself is a thorax—chaos,
a peninsular punctuation on the edges
to inns of stables, of mangers and of pools…

With the blood on the road gray colors
hunt for shadows of malarial fear. How is it
that the soldier is threatened by clinical silence
and the guerilla tormented by the wilderness?

On the grass is the mother who drinks
the blood of her breasts, eats the bones of her
babies before taking the road. She's not aware
that every refuge is a font. The road opens
its hunger hiccupping and belching the gas
of mixed blood sandwiched by stampeding trees.

NIGHT SHADOWS

Night shadows have shaped
my thoughts ever since I gave myself
to the crocodile in my Sierra Leone;
and my brothers too have written me mad
in the palms of our dead; the same

Brothers I dueled with and stabbed
in a dark room where they idled and hungered
for the flesh of the sister. I lived in the communes
before I got imprisoned in four walls; I stood
the suicidal ground to fight my country`s shapeless
course; I cruised the peninsula's thorax through
lost horizons to discover the Shangri-La where no bitter
cross awaited my songs and poetry, and
where I enjoyed my forefathers'
voices in bright fireplaces

The brothers who plotted my life
were children of my father's;
they said my tongue had become
fratricidal since condemning
my soul to that of Frantz Fanon,
who turn over in his grave with
other wretched of the earth. I pounded
the floor of my prison

between the labyrinthine network
of my life and my country`s
forgotten revolutionaries after
my excreta and I survived
the treachery of the parasites
who came to me serpiginous.
I have overcome it all because poetry is now
what I am. From my small window
I caution the younger brother. And ever
since the reptilians sent me their animal signal that I am
being waylaid at water places, I have not stopped
versifying inside this belly of the crocodile.

THE DINING TABLE

Dinner tonight comes with
gun wounds. Our desert
tongues lick the vegetable
blood—the pepper
strong enough to push scorpions
up our heads. Guests
look into the oceans of bowls
as vegetables die on their tongues.

The table
that gathers us is an island where guerillas
walk the land while crocodiles
surf. Children from *Alphabeta* with empty palms dine
with us; switchblades in their eyes,
silence in their voices. When the playground
is emptied of children`s toys
who needs roadblocks? When the hour
to drink from the cup of life ticks,
cholera breaks its spell on cracked lips

Under the spilt
milk of the moon, I promise
to be a revolutionary, but my Nile, even
without tributaries comes lazy
upon its own Nile. On this

night reserved for lovers of fire, I'm
full with the catch of gun wounds, and my boots
have suddenly become too reluctant to walk me.

THE DRAWING BOARD

Since the newscast on the tick of ten
tsetse flies have been buzzing
the four walls of this room. Why must
sadness roll like wind after such a vigil with
the clock? Papers are shuffling
to protest the weight of a dumb elephant
that suddenly sits idly on the green
carpet grass. It had started with mosquitoes,
why has it turned to flies, and then
to an elephant? Whoever cleared and gathered the filth
at the outside door is aware of the metamorphosis
inside the room. And now our pages are empty of ink
save the portrait of an elephant sitting on the grass
"This meeting is over? Go back
and wake up your dead. Tell them
we achieved the elephant. I will make
a Xerox copy for each of you. But first I'd like
to catch the buzzing flies oozing off the elephant's
ears whispering in our ears something about
the sun hanging over the roof."

I'VE NEVER KNOWN THAT IN THE LAND OF THE DEAD CHILDREN ARE BORN, THOUGH I KNOW DEAD PEOPLE IDLE IN BED

Like a drunkard I stumble
upon a mirror in the graveyard, in the full
view of others' barbed wired scars; no light
in my head to show me how the dead give
birth to their dead. Corpses, with the sorrow
of their many faces drink *gbangbang*,[4] their blood
banked in bat's jaws to merge with green spirits
retreating to earth-oblivion on the stumps of imaginary
forests, where it was rumored the dead once hung
their cloaks and lost them. The moon covers
my feet bringing to me the memory of my being alive
in the company of my dead brothers. I see
the rude scars of the graveyard's teeth. Further
along as I leap out of ghostly shadows baby corpses
beckon to me; from beneath them comes the smell of myrrh.

---

[4] *Gbangbang: bitter medicinal herbs*

72

FRAUDSTER

You came charging
through our streets on
a pillion the day we had powers
to dance on pieces of broken bottles;
you conjured silver linings
from the reflection of the sea
and polythenes of echoes to break
open the coastal rocks of our heroes' potency;
you swarm in the air in ethereal bliss
condemning us to your poltergeist-self
whipping your hurried looks upon us
through requiems; you hid your mortal wounds
from us suffering in your foolery O Salmoneus!

The megalomania of being a magician
the magic of being megalomaniac.
You who have no hands in the trinity
came breaking through the skies
of our calendar, not able to comprehend
the diptych and the triptych;
and when the hurricane came
your own gaze deceived you;
the tumbling waves and the rupture
tearing into your chariot planted
in the blindness of our sights the clouds of Zeus.

OFFSHOOT

Of late the boy has grown
taller than a tree. His eyes
stick out from a bushy forest on his head
monitoring the distance between himself
and the rest of us. Power lies across
his back with its tunnel of thunder
rolling on the corridor of his youth. Once

He carried his mother's kitchen on his head
to fill the void his father left in the bedroom—at that
time the wind had swept their roof and had flown away
with all their umbilical cords buried
in the foundation. His narcotic father had laughed
at the darkness and the swaying of the stern
of his household—he would not be seen talking
to shadows leaning on trees when he should
be tying them up with ropes. So when against
the bitter tears of his better half
and at the break of light when the shadows

Had vanished, he pursued them. As a child the boy
remembers that all too well—of a father dropping the void
on his mother's husband and trapping a whole marriage inside

a calabash. That was too much to meet with: a simple
kitchen built with forest firewood. How come his father
didn't realize he was raising a family on coal? There was

Also the porch where the flowers had perished; and
under the bench his father was used to sitting on
was the rotten gourd of palm wine he and his friends
had thundered over like a cool jury accessing
the cases of blood in the lips of their victims.

ELEGY

When hot blood runs
down our globular heads,
pressing against our eternal valleys,
sipping and cascading through
our defenseless black follicular strands,
and draining into our couched palms,
this kingdom's frontier soldiers
fortified by banana mountains,
where kings and subjects
sleep the livelong day—a
kingdom inhaling rude stilettos
is buried in the haunch of monotonous
wind. When smoky hearts journey the world,
the silent and bloodless faces of the sun
turn yellow then colorless.

WALL

My brother
who died in the war
came to me in my dream
smelling my armpits. Disgusted

I blew his face, wanting to observe his dangling
shadow hanging loosely in the air.

He came in calico, his feet
turning over the soil from which I saw
my own testament. It was a dark hour
in a bright day, and all the mourning flowers

Had been dunked. With my accustomed
faces, I idled in the deep curve. My brother

Who died in the war, shoved out of my dream
to listen to the dirges of yellow flowers. I chose
to view fallen branches in the new empire
of the commonweal, built
between dream and memory to this day.

SLEEVES

for the mutilated by those with mutilated minds

The long and short of it—
a college of gods has fallen
for mutation. Shooting themselves
in the head they dug out their brains
and fired their imaginations; plucked
out their eyes and filled the sockets
with torches heliacal of blood pressured stars.

They fell from heaven and
occupied my country inconveniencing
the calendar days; they hated nudity
atavistic of Adam and Eve's; sought
to correct heaven with sleeves—
the long and short of it shaped
on the arms of my countrypeople.

SOLITUDE AFTER WAR

The kinship between tree and branch
has changed; a brace of independence
characterizes the green spirits
in between. I no longer have to worry

About nightlines of fireflies
in the woods. My chasm that is to say
my hunger will not strike me again
as worms. Yesterday I sat under
the Cotton Tree to ponder
on the parable of the cup and today
the flood is real: the rain washed off
mud when dinosaurs had a flat earth
all to themselves. Mangy dogs scattered
in our streets confronted men, pearls

Chained to their necks. Yesterday after
our forested women encountered Socrates
in their paths, and drank his hemlock
from inside his transparent oesophagus
they desired the death-wish
of dining with madmen who fed

On desert locusts; after which they seduced
the young people of the city, screaming delirious

theories—a cadaverous body of knowledge
whose folios were tucked under their breasts:

the feathers of tomorrow's dinosaurs
the reptilian thirst of man to evolve
and how our shadows shall inherit the earth

The other day the weatherman
announced the return of the storm
darkened with locusts just after these
women had carved new gods to watch
over their college caped in their peninsula.

As a child of those haunted capes, I have not
forgotten the tablets on the hills of temper;
each night fragmented calabashes crack
underneath the breasts of the Amazons.

Wolves and jackals have taken to crying
in my head; and in the morning when I step
out telephone wires strangle me. Why
must I be haunted by wailing from empty
canoes? I try to trace my bitter river to familiar
landscapes, to fill my glass with its wine of solitude
but all I get is the hush sound of its running water.

HILLS OF TEMPER

I rose above the Rokel searching
for my name rushed into the Congo
banks where Tchikaya U Tams'i washed
his French wounds; into Mongo Park's Niger
where other black Saharan poets, bleaching
in their anger over the gushing waters
stood as attentive as ever to the brewing
storm like a fowl with one leg raised.

Among us poets—also brothers
a color lost our umbilical cords in the dust
where our mother dipped her fingers shedding
the tears she always wanted to shed, renting
her hair over the taproot she always watered.

I gathered my sheaf in the eleven
hands of my mother's harvest, dreaming
of a journey into the ethos of my country
talking as a poet to those who were also poets,
tasting the pus the bitter side of my Sierra Leone.

Between my soul and my days I fought
to reconcile two metaphorical images,
the result was an enslaved child and a Babel of tongues,
and there I sat between the living Warawara stones

81

searching to hunt the lions of Pedro Da Cintra
or the drinking skulls of the Portuguese entrepreneurs
who stretched my mother in the winter market of Lisbon.

My name was lost in a feud of waves. I found
the truth in some English graves buried
in the shadows of my poisoned blood
through which I photographed their young
men: atavistic images destroying my manchild.

My bitterness became my light, my light
the landscape in my head as I assumed the phoenix
rising to soar above the conspiracy of the Amistad.

PHILOSOPHY & WATER

For the three stones on Wusum Hills, Makeni

Keeping vigil
of silence in mediaeval
nudity, the backs of these three large
stones overlooking Makeni, have broken
many tablets and now embrace the *kaaba*
ciborium of blood. They have shed
their granite skins on man—the lake
that licks on mud edges. Peasants lay
their hearts full of blood on the gruesome
porcelains of their empty sacks.

Trapped within a silent body of knowledge
In the pages of the many scrolls leafed by the wind
they berth to witness locusts plaguing
on mortality—man and rock
sweaters of the universe and
conquerors of fire, have, with their embrace
ever existed protected by a common
element: the rock next time, the man next time.

So in the after-blood
of my country, and on the corpses
of my country people, if I'm unable
to reach my tributary, I'll smear my bloody
hands on the three rocks of Wusum Hills.

83

REJUVENATE ME

I have suffered the ideologies
of men while searching for corner
stones on all the mountains I know; while searching
for drinking water in all the rivers I know; in distant
eyes I have seen insufficiency stitched on the macabre

looks of nightly stars; in the morning of my torment
I look at my neighbor's face—it is a mausoleum
of voiceless scars. Passing by lakes
in days gone by the men of solitude
loomed large in my library—their psychedelic
views I danced into like thrown stones
splashing the lake's acid of prurience
on every one of our pregnant women; and

so every year new babies seek apples even
before age five—learn to flatter angels,
seeking temptation from behind the dianthus,
my euphemistic mortality—I laugh at the enclosing
cave. Gorgeous I march reneging into my twentieth

century renovating broken cisterns, subversive
of the painful papyrus of Grecian scrolls;
subservient to new gods of the wastage
of my ointment. I am the paprika of my age, in

the soul of my light was planted a pungent
seed and my father's faith filled my mother's
womb. Naked I come, illustrious, the ignominious
apple in the throat. Immerse me into my father's
sperm and my mother's mastoid breasts.

REIGNING IN BLOOD

Green grass is crying
Frightened weeds gather under
Fine grass outgrows the weeds
The weeds die under

Savannah Pride wallows on buffalo waste
to fool its prey and beat back its sense of smell
in same way the common man is kept at bay
even as the republic disintegrates in his bed,
all captured in broken mirrors of canine teeth; and
heartburns, constipation and sour grapes.

Poised with grumbling bellies and fallen bottoms
and innards of rotten materials, the land
dries up in the wake of droughts and doubts;
the seasons miscalculate in their calendar days
and no bird with horticultural pronouncement
flies the skies with twigs between its beaks.

Our politicians are moths, wind-blown into mud
who wriggle on the ground and die without
the mastery of dance to the impeccable night drums
and bleeding fingers that do the drumming;
and when their moons occasionally eclipse incorporeal,
groping shadows poise in faltered steps to overthrow.

LET ME SPEAK FOR MYSELF

I am Sierra Leone,
the hurricane of my birth
perches on my razed edges,
the cortege of my children glazes
the hands of the colonial shadows. In the middle
passage the dolor is two; and I forfeit
all clement duality hence the preservation
of the self. Pedro Da Cintra scares me
with imaginary lions, and I wedge my mouth
in the O of my torment,
spanning in my silence;
and though I crisscross Pedro with a double-edged
sword, yet my children drink of his life's cerebral
wine; and now I suffer a baptism in the very hands
of my children—
they call it a renewal
of my soul. I call it the wax replenishing
the agony of my ashen sky;
occasionally I utter a wilderness of laughter
wherever I cannot creep the tuberous mountain
of extensional influence; and as long as I keep converting
myself I shall be the amoebic sister. I shape
and reshape my cartographic concept,
and I mirror the great resolves of faraway places
in the clearing skies. Because I mourn my heart, I'm going
through fjords in garments meant for widows.

OUR DEVELOPED MEN

Our developed men
are growing well into night shadows
where firmaments promise them gods
dressed in blue jeans like a sea.

Contretemps!

Contumacious men of cow dung
dream, sleep and dream trees of it;
and because we don't know such dreams
in the consumption class, we leave them
in their cities and go into the woods,
into the muscles of the forests to conjure
the conundrum of their scary faces.

There are gods in our developed men,
jealous gods who couldn't be told about
a past world locked in camwood leaves.

And these gods using the anuses of our developed
men, fart into the lungs of our breath to suffocate
the huge men among us, huge men with deep
breath whom we call super humans or deformed
gods—men with whom
the gods have scores to settle.

Grallatorial birds come singing this mishap
into the ears of the cattle in grassland kiosks
telling prophesies of doom; and we children
of shepherds hear some of it and question
our parents who lie helplessly six feet below us.
After which we sit on cross-roads and cross
our legs because that is all we could do.

ROETHKE WRITES

Roethke writes, *I may be some time,*
I hang over his "snake"
witnessing the reincarnation in him.
At once I want to write the crucifixion,
taking the story back
to undo the genesis tale,
man the man killer
in the erection of pre-Adamite men.

Alone I strike
moderating my steps on his pergola,
reflecting the universal transgression, man to man.
Again I strike holding my fragile
soul between dark nights and pathless rocks,
experiencing the reality of head and heel crushing
to the rhythm if the course,
to the rhythm of the curse,
man the man killer.

So shall it be,
man submitting himself
to himself,
in parks,
in coffee shops,
in temples,

in alcoves.
Roethke in our shadows
crouch bellywise
at our doorsteps.

ORDINARY MAN

I am an ordinary man in town
who walks on the sides of supermen
but keeps away from their palms
because I am ordinary man with eyesight
able to see the whiteness sprouting
in my countrypeople's skull.

I am an ordinary man in town
who occupies a place in everyman's eyes,
who sets their nerves in motion. I speak and
write their lips' language dominated
by voiceless bilabial plosives,
provoked by societal lavas.

I am an ordinary man in town
who laughs with my tongue between my teeth,
my teeth between my gums,
hermitic poor lips.

PREACHER

Merely smoothening palm against palm,
merely drilling them till they blaze,
merely juxtaposing screaming fingers,
sweeps a thousand feet a thousand miles away.

O woman in yesterday's void
wriggling and ranting over castrated poets,
merely nailing the cross on my brother's stony head
and stony feet, merely bludgeoning your vocal cords
with streams of air will not do.

You do well smoothening fingernails against
fingernails, upholding the tempered hills
of Nazareth perambulating with Rachel
weeping within the breasts of crouching caves.

You do well cannibalizing the blood
of a mutilated giant; you thud men's hearts
on the hard cover of the sacred anthology
but the structure of the road to the Christian forest
is the devil's point of argument.

I CLIMB THE HEIGHT OF DAY

I climb the height of day
using both hands and legs
leaving behind amoebic shadows
to inherit their lights.

I set my eyes on the hills
thinking about the struggle
between soul and flesh.

I count the seasons of *kiribambe* in my land
before I begin my journey
breaking through upturned calabashes.

Between abandoned shadows and empty corpses
are seasons of anomy.

I multiply my moments of night watch
while I struggle to wave from my head
the being of shadows and windows.

I figure my proportion
while I measure the height of day; this
is why I keep thinking
of casting my body to the valley's crocodile
whose hope of survival I share.

I hear someone shouting
that I am acting against my own interest;
at once I know that if anyone looks like me I aught
to declare that we are both children of separation.
Some time ago a friend told me that in climbing
One can find oneself take a nautical plunge.

But I have learnt to stand my ground
firmly trying to prove him wrong
even if I should meet my ocean,
the measurement of height
while climbing the acme of day.

The wind is my measuring rod laid lengthily
across each day's crucible. Man perishes not
in climbing the height, but in experiencing
his life's patches while measuring.

Those who have learnt to wring their fingers
at the altitude of fear have shifted my faith
an inch since my phobia of height.
To them that say, "He's ambitious" I return word
for word the edge of being Sierra Leonean
while fighting to reclaim that which leaves can't absorb.

The journey sweetens the pain,
the pain strengthens the hope,
and at this point it becomes clear to me
that I am moving toward the window
of my shadow's ambition.

MILTON MARGAI TEACHERS COLLEGE

Such a place lingers like a shadow
and crumbles like log-fires into ashes of concepts
inside the head that just begins to grow hair.

Like a wounded grass it pours white-grey
the sum total of life.

The frog dance does not last long
where green leaves sprout
and divide their blades to become pages.

The sea rolls her scrolls
unto the dark campus for young castaways
who search in the dark seeing life in death; and
in their madness they break stones like nuts
looking at the inner side with green gazes.

Lamps blaze in Harmattans
when they are not threatened by laden winds
and now I sing like desert birds,
plying routes between oases.

Such a place lingers like shadows
and as I walk in the light
it sheds from my image to linger with me.

MY EYES ARE NO MIRROR

They look at the whole of you
behind your black skin,
beyond your new name
rooted in the baobab tree,
behind your grand ancestor's hut
and tell you when the gods
shall meet to exile you.

My eyes look beyond shadows
to see and study reflections
of all black twins,
bathed in stagnant water
and tell whom the gods so love.

My eyes see the first wind
that blows against new black babies
and know what they leave with them
and what they take from them.

My eyes look between parents
and see how many seeds are there,
how many will germinate.

My eyes are no mirror,
these eyes that watch the African
landscape each black night
with torches burning
behind nocturnal elements.

AND THESE SHALL BE THE SIGNS

You may know that in December
The year ends.

It is always at this time
That pictures sink behind calendars.

This is not like refreshing notions
Where one thought replaces another in the mind.

In December the African November spills shards
Of night silver and this has always helped shaped

The way you and everyone here has learnt
To bend the helm.

But there is a bitter jungle where darkness
Has found no respite and in this jungle no bush grows.

However, don't compare it with a desert in wind-clashed
Seasons where the tallest object is not safe.

Only in a lamb's eyes can such similes be seen;
There in its eyes you will see the silver thread,

The harbinger of October tragedies
Of wayfarers of travelers born when the earth was flat.

Many people are victimized in this penumbra
Of life while seeking the great resolve between life and
death.

Once a poet dared to cry within the walls of her realm
Where an asphalt tree grew and bent over her pages,

Where she had written herself in verses of Latin
And cried for want of understanding.

You might not have witnessed how as a surrealist
I have really suffered the hypocrisy of civilization

Now listen to the church bells

Which now throb in city centers
Where the gods kill supermen.

Good riddance?

Here and there a tin-god of chameleon descent
Thrusts his leg in the throats of the people's hope

Right in the parks where these supermen
Feed pigeons whose minds are set on trapping angels.

Yes, there was once a man in Africa
Born before his time. I don't know where in Africa,

Since all the mountains look alike and crouch
Without the need for a continent to be named Freetown.

The man it was said lamented before he died
That he wished our gods were not eternal.

He feared we shall have them around
Plotting to edge us off our grounds

"And these shall be the signs," he said. "Your mountains
Shall no more crouch nor roast your lambs with fire!"

TO SAY THE LEAST

For Lt. Nabie Lamin Kargbo, KIA

It was the milk of the moon
we fed on that evening
to show our joy for his recruitment. We had it
flowing our eyes,
and he with his calabash at hand
bent over to gather our generosity; we meant it,
that was why we gave him well. We pushed him,
disrobing him of his name
wearing on him
the withering leaves of Sierra Leone; we lied to him,
that we were covering his shame
we lied to him
we did,
echoing our promises
with our heads buried over his calabash,
supported by his trembling hands; we begged him
not to graduate,
before him we stood
the skeleton of those who graduated years
before and showed him the areas where their shadows
took possession of them. "But you will be
shadow free. You will be purged of that dark
pigment, that dark dye." He braved it all from the window
of his bliss where the fratricidal
shadow took possession of him.

TO A BROKEN OMOLANKAY

The woodcutter's labor
Wound a creation from a needle's eye
Pricked joints for life locomotion
With thrust arms to obey Newton's law.

A whole creation with a difference,
Like I look beyond the naked keys of a piano
Or like I converse with a drummer
And a pianist over wine.

This deep waterless sea drowns
Every fisherman's, every market woman's,
Every farmer's, every miner's,
And at sunset fish them, farm them,
Market them to the people.

You are familiar with the city
Why dumb here
Where the daily rubbish is sieved.
Down at Paterson Zochonis
Men and women lose their necks,
Taxi drivers hoot their horns laughing.
Rise again old boy,
Your dues are paid to the FCC.

See your inscription holds,
A man only dies.
Run with your living wheels,
The city is going dark!

I SING OF MEN I PITY

Silver waves crouch
unto the shores of human misery,
enveloping eggs of pain of women,
breaking on beaches of sorrow
in the pain of death,
in the death of pain,
poets will sing in blank verses
and free lyrics.

A song like mine
composed on the clash of mortars
and pestle this gloomy July, God knows what hour

I sing the rage of the sea,
the gnarl of August of human misery,
walking between the parapet of time and age.

To many the moon,
trapped in the cobweb of the sun
is not capable of having a name.

The most frustrating men
to whom the grasp of divine poetry
is unachievable in the reading of their palms
have submitted themselves stark naked

to the night I am running away from.
These lugubrious men stand against the raging
sea to see it vomit its belly contents.

COUNTRYPEOPLE

Wake up from your slumber
and behold the refulgent eyes of your moons
that cry over your starving seas. How can you endure
this malaise when a million unicellular organisms

Up from dead flesh ginger you in your
heliotrope world? O men of helical fame,
herbivores of the henbane,
running around in circles
circling in circles,

Let me show you the quintessence of the mimosa
spreading flowers over the evergreen land.

As I speak to you,
the edges of the world
are tormented by our fratricidal relationship.

SHE CARRIES IT ON HER HEAD SIDEWAYS

She carries it on her head
sideways along the single path
of green and brown
which snakes the future of her legs.

Far ahead the old sun
shapes her a new day
on the heads of tall trees
whose within couch simple ideas
refreshed by green leaves
in her cloying Sierra.

She has no mind of hers
to follow; all she does is take
the autocratic road,
like all operational women
she walks in and out of her ingrowing
memory inconspicuously.

Over the years
she has formed an island
with an insularity of shaded views
and its invertebrate myth
curl inward rising to equal her myopia.

Her weary life of calabash breaks in shreds,
and she gather the bits under her soft breath,
and on its broken map
she begins another journey on the ghostly
weft of the long jagged sierra.

RUPTURE

for Dele Charley

The rupture tore my heart
like a successful flash in the dark,
and I looked unto the crouching hills
of my Sierra Leone where Dele's blood
boiled in an alcove to achieve his single testimony.

I saw the flash of life
in my emptiness as my ravished soul
groped in the body cosmos,
searching for my country's voice
strangled by a thread from the river.

I saw the river transporting raw calabashes
under several broken bridges where I lost Salia's voice,
strangled in ring-waves and that of Rogie's
now coming to me like a tired sea.

As Dele sipped Kolosa's tears in my eyes
the Rokel surged into my free land
undressing my Sierra Leone.

The Rokel swept away the green calabashes
of my countrymen, and I was left standing on the lonely shore
dead- awake—my voice struggling to ascend the stars.

111

And I suddenly wished I could berate the sea for its fake gold on which I stood. I turned to the wind which I knew tormented the sea and I cried, "O match flare wind, why did you obfuscate me in this theatre like the night call of *the blood of a stranger*?"

IN HIS MEMORY
For Yaya Kanu

I held a leaf in memory of his pain. I cannot
remember its color because it did not last long
in my sleep.

A strong hurricane blew it away and settled
its remains where trees interlock, shaping
the rays of the sun and the waters
of the sea.

I saw its weakness in my sleep
and my heart pounced
in the middle of the night.

Live! Live! Live!

A voice cried all night long.

Hurry, hurry into the forest
and turn the mirror's face to the wall

Again my heart pounced
as the voice urged me on.

It was painful;
the morning night strangled the voice

and a heavy rain beat my conscience wet
thudding in my guilt.

Don't wait you Negro!

In the dark I hid my shadow
fighting my days in his days
and his days in my days.

I saw a sharp darkness
as his light went off
reverberant darkness,
black revulsion,
colorless convulsion—pain running
my eyes like a child's nose. And I heard
the voice again:

Bestride fields of yellow leaves
where old calabashes squat,
consider this your challenge
in this Harmattan season.

I wanted someone to close this chapter,
to stop the cold blood leaching through
my fruitless quietness.

LET US MAKE A YELLOW JOKE

For Isioma Daniels

Let us make a yellow joke about
our political leaders even if we risk
waking up the reptiles in them to fly
their dark chromes in mucky skies to play God.

Now we want our independence, and
we should say, asking of it with spitting fumes
and without liturgy—WE ARE ASKING!

These one- eyed one-life giants are
blind and empty of caves in their hearts.

The earth eats, the cold earth
eats, they forget too soon; the soil
browns with vegetable flesh,
they forget too soon.

Let us say to them,
don't play god on us!

Let us say to them that
our backs have carried their behinds
for too long; and that our woes are filled with
the echoes of their peninsular laughter while
our outrageous bamboo thatch catch

fire from the riverbeds in our city centers; that we
want our landscapes back, void of their finger-prints.
let us ask them to withdraw their morning
dews from our puritanical emblem. Let us say
we have seen their kinds in the dust of viral flight.

Die Dictators, die! Africa
hungers for a birthday!

The red charcoal of time is coaxing
the lion inside of us; don't play god
on the mane. Mandela is alive like grown immortals
and in the stones of cadaverous Sese Sekou
and now life is painful from your yellow
bite. How many more bull dogs must
we let out to lap dry the water of the Nile and
shatter the rocks of Kilimanjaro? You murdered
N'krumah before we had time to read his manual;
your dark branches strangled Lumumba by the neck
hanging his mackintosh on a deformed stump.

Africa shall never suffer the wagon of the quick
smell of your farewell. Patriarchal of evolution,
it was the continent that popped up the flint
and bound itself on both sides with the ghosts
of its perished gods. *Go, good do!*

THREADING THE VOID

Boy child bathed in flood
water that rips his ribs creating a language
for him to cry in; girl child

born with apple green eyes; garden leaves
rattle on their branches while yellow
flowers coil in serpentine bliss. It follows

that the boy and girl
need a big bang and a black hole
to attain the astronomical on the back

of a crocodile clutching the splintered
rocks; a chameleon to tame
the time between
the beginning and the end; so that when

the sun throws its finger into the air and grabs
clocks by their ticking arms, the moon

rises grey and paint brushes
the sky where souls shroud in coffin; the stars
die and burn in the belly; it rains
and washes the Nile and the Mississippi
writing histories upon their silt; thunder

117

quakes and drills into the man-child. The cyclone
spirals and scrapes the roof of the sky when the gods
mate between rocks of clouds. And in the silence,
mists dusting off this chaos, and relaxing
the muscles of the gods
help us behold…

WATERFRONT

Yesterdays are narrow. Let us come out
of them. Let us leave behind us the shadows
from whose bodies we would leap like
a kangaroo so that we become
gods to crack open the skulls of tin-gods
of angels of horns. Before we emerge
from the dark water they imprisoned us,
the stones carrying our weights must all
be sunk into the ocean; or shall we erect them concave-like
to trap down their divinity? Ahead of us are frequent
deserts to which we must be equal, otherwise, thirsty
in their solitude the tin-gods like starved dogs will lap
our sweats. They catch our whispers in the wind;
cringe green philosophies with the smell
of dead fish scales in their oases. We must
be steadfast birds in the air because their thoracic
deserts have no blue horizons to catch glimpse
of us soaring in the sky. Let us fly over pictures
of sandstorms. And like eagles, scatter the knuckles
of yellow camels, so that we may come
out free of claws and long scars
to fly over other landscapes where
our eyes would uphold painless waterfronts.

IN THE DEEP RECESSES OF HUNGER

Your trinkets blur on imaginary
corpses in the water,
to redesign heaven on
the shoulders of the earth.
I approach you to watch
your mind, but you keep clinging
to the miracles of your bangles.
You have no eyes on your face;
and you deny earth her clear skies.
You seek for new opening
but already your shadow
is eating into your brain. I must warn you
once your entrails can no longer
fire an imagination
the angels will dress your shadows with trinkets
and you will be damned
when you come to know this new art
the gods have learnt to kill.
So let your trinkets
stay in the water. Who can move
the heavens to brim their banks?
Let not your shadow
break calabashes. There is a desert
in landlocked heaven;
the men who have gone through it

have reported bodies planted mid air
waiting for a gravitational force.

WE NO LONGER WRITE POEMS IN CAMERA

No longer do we write poems in camera
with helicopters hovering over our heads
enervating the sticking fingers of our branches
which like the Sierra now stands unkempt.

Illogical though we may seem like languages
falling down Babel our poems are read all over
the place. From Freetown to Conakry where the
malarial mosquito expends; from Rwanda to Soweto
where black blood illustrates the future before each
liquid surges to fill helpless skeletons.

We have not quarreled with anyone only that we know
poems too have enemies, thus they have sworn
to stand enormous, renting the pages of houses
we build them. We wish human skins were pachydermatous
like those of our brothers on veranda hammocks
who continue to feel they are forever separated from
the verse they refuse to write; the skins of the mother
who in secret mash formless bones depriving
the marsupial land incarnate voices.

We have scribbled a dozen poems in the Sahara
all to be read in black capitals: from Dakar
to Yaoundé; Libreville to Kinshasa, down the uneven

ribs of Kigali; from Nairobi to Monrovia; Kampala
to Mogadishu, unto the drooping shadows of
Ouagadougou.

A stanza for the creeping Congo
A metaphor for Mauritius
An ankle for Angola
A mail for Ivory Coast
A poet for Africa!

PORTRAIT

Tonight we are going to be missing
from their eyes. But you and I know
where we stand foiled in the thick coat of the evening
which daily emerges from the true color
of mountain stones. Already I can see the stumps
beside their soles; very soon they stumble upon us,
"Oh, you are almost invisible!" they say. They know
we are invisible each time we come home
to roost. Not 'almost, 'we are a part of the evening.

When we wear our evening dresses
we turn into iron-one,' our shiny
elements bulge our eyes;
our silver stands up to oceanic blue—colored aristocracy
on piano banquet. Their stares burn into our flesh,
as their celebrated artists paint us
in the sky with fire in their eyes.

Tonight is our primordial vigilance as we watch
how their artists spill our images. Do you see
the morphology of our heads—two shadows and no
objects? Your chest is hidden behind my shoulder
and my brawn upsetting my head—wild feet on desert
sand—mouth large with noisy teeth—plein-air images
against a void background.

HARMATTAN

Night forth, terra cotta daylight
on my two- same creatures of a peninsular
ego: one leaping into the multi-graffiti
wind, another gnarling for the blue
taste of the sea; both wing'd
to battle the thorax of my desert
for a passage to the melting
dawn. This is the crisscross of a storm
knelt in the heart with piercing teeth
that make overblown shadows shiver. I suffer

a centrifugal disagreement
with my two-same. Between
the blue sea and the multi-graffiti wind lies
a premature sepulcher . The air's dry laughter
slashes the lips of the scorching sun,
its blood infecting the abdomen
of day, sedating the tasteless sweats
of my riverside spirits. This moment
feels like a stump and my universe
begins to experience a radiation
sexual of the sun. I am divided
between the painful languages
of the earth; the sun is buoyant perpendicular
to its swollen lips. My four eyes are wet

125

with castor-oil surrealistic of my
agony. The sun fears its black hole but burns
open my layers. I seek a labyrinthine
trap to set it against its own
energy that I may stitch my split-man
with dynamics: earth, wind and fire. But who
will blindfold it while I web a heptagon? Apollo
duelling with time has cut off the ancient
veins of the stars. In a place
where daggers have met with arrows
for a decade, children are born with lighting
on their tongues. I sit on a limestone
to crack open thunders in the heads
of these child-victims, but a crippled god
from neon miles muscles himself
into their brains, erasing the molecular
linguistics only chaos can form. In my anger
I wish a Medusa on my shoulder with Joshua
eyes. The sun must be quenched
in circular curves with desert sand
to turn to stone the face of an awkward
decade. I awake upon a mound
with a new terra cotta dawn; the sun, too, like
the earth has a new dress: One picking
steps of cavalcade, the other greying with the shadow
hiccupping in flooded coasts. I see the crippled god

in the company of other gods, Kissing
the brainless skulls of children
made electronic on the weight of this new season
carried on the back of a tortoise behind the colorless
chameleon that is my country.

POET UNWANTED

Agony is his name
who materializes from a sheep's blare
after a false census that didn't register poets.

That census was organized to seek edge-sword
men for whom the Stephen stone has been
stolen from the museum.

Gates are keyed with the beam
of night moons and are open only to those
who profess to hate the lines of poetry
running across the sky-scape like lighting.

There are men trained to wait at the foot of the gates
at the expense of their own lives
as long as they spill the blood of poets
in thirsty vineyards.

Out in the desert where men bathe
in blood I'm told to fuck-off and use the sun's
mouth if I must shout.

while I stab my heart in their sorrow, their women
open up their legs to me and ask if I would drink
the contents from a sponge.

Their wish is to liquidize me while
I remind them of Golgotha; to have me plunged
headward in the sea of commonplace.

They sip my blood in their laughter and laugh
at my supper of grasshopper
but fail to see their deaths
as they dovetail in my filial eyes.

A bird has been flying in my head
provoking me on the fortieth
year of my patience, but I still opt
to cast the bread of my hunger
to the vultures while I drink the
water of the oases where I go
every Sunday to watch a million
billows without an eye blink.

A LONG WALK HOME

Hill hunch hill,
yesterday's exile sobbing
and weeping
fast forward and weeping
against their backs and
talking muscles; with

weighty corpses in their eyes which refuse
to melt into tears even
when tear-dried eyes brim; with

shadows pressing on them
from behind; unreflecting thorn
scars, white palms
of dark blood and flesh. Exile
supporting exile like bouncing
balls; and the big toes
of their bare soles weigh

the narrow path home; wet
ground and compact soil,
wanting the pressure *hum hum*
the quiet breath of the dead;
withered air of agony; more
corpses keep arriving for God

to house. On this path sandwiched
by bleeding graves dissident angels
come in the night to fuck yellow
prostitutes who walk the road as nuns.

HARVEST

We made our reports
but no one listened to us
so we poured ashes on our heads
and tore our garments into two
sending one toward the orient.

We withdrew our hands to cover
our nakedness—hands of creepy
joints journeyed back with sweats
our left hands came freezing.

We nursed them till they gave
on our right arms were serrations
our veins were breathing belching
thick and sticky white foams
our left arms bore tattoos but
the black designs would not tell.

WHEN THE CLOUDS BECOME TOO THICK

Long prismatic legs walk the streets
marching in their millions with no void
left for human steps—bouncing
though with no boots to protect
their feet…bare feet on tarmac
lanes and winding paths,
rivers, hills and forests too.

Bruising leaves and flowers
which refuse to dance to the
drumming zinc covering the thatch
and silver tins idling in their heavens.

A *shegureh*[5] beat at a counterpoint
with drumming hiccupping in tidal
crescendo in virgin forests accompanying
the chorale of children never to be born
to this earth. Their song continue to be
heavy on the thick muscles of gathering clouds.

And just before the end, there
is always a crepuscular hailstorm
echoing base voices owned
by men who once inhabited
the earth when it was flat.

---

[5] *Tambourine*

GREAT SCARCIES, LITTLE SCARCIES

Morning sun upturns tin-dog's *jaygay*[6]
eyes run blood like *okuru*[7] dog's,
filthy *kasankay*[8] shame mourners;
light approaches but time gnarls
a denial; asexual morning buds
open psyches of early flowers
but dark wind sinks clairvoyant
pollens of life forms; red moons
evanesce into ice-thoughts
exacerbating into neglect
the premonition of emotions. Between

the Great Scarcies and the little Scarcies
my generation seeks to silence
every tin-god; it is otherwise
known as the Scarcies resolve
that would burn the stars and spray
the ashes where sea and sky stitch
thickening their grey matter
as new babies learn to swim in the fresh
water of the firmament. Up from the ashes
of burnt days log-fires flame, roasting

---

[6] *shell*
[7] *mangy*
[8] *shroud*

flesh in wombs pushing out
babies dressed in blue jeans. A noon
like that of Joshua waits long for men

whose women stand as pillars of salt;
machines drink and hiccup blood;
new babies suck the breasts of fine
terra cotta corpses; the wounded dogs bark
like sea waves licking with rage very
much like that of the medusa. Poets,
with their cameras poised hope to capture
a moment to shoot back verses into
fratricidal and other hearts, and to urge
spent legs into the womb of Sierra Leone.

OF WINDOWS AND SHADOWS

...eventually they lose their skins
and co-exist with conformity

The windows of the ambivalent ones shall
remain open creating vexing scenes that make
them rude with their shadows flashing teeth
of canine shapes that saunter deep
into our wounded souls. The ambivalent
ones stand in mucky alcoves holding back every
facial expression. They create moments that

carve deserts in our thoraxes, stabbing holes
in our hearts to deprive us of oases. We journey
into our Harmattan seeking the winding
roads to their bleak faces to talk sense

to them; but with their shadows supporting them
they escape to their windows leaving us to be
deafened by the rude monsoon. We rage in our
anger at their weightless laughter that echoes inside
us eating the hunger that is keeping us alive.

ON THEIR BLINDNESS

...the fear of immigrants swamping
European culture and eventual "browning"
of the West by people of darker pigmentation.

-West Africa, 1993

Even though
for humans and animals
all holes hang, I'm surprised
to learn that the parable refuses
to journey through shaped rains and
suns to achieve Shangri-La;

Or is it that men refuse to be
or are they unable to convert
such a parable to technology
or at least to wind?

But even so,
what good when such winds
we talk of wear skins
laminated with theories of the universe
through blown trees and macabre deserts.

137

The wind
through its crucibles
sheds its white color
to suck the green pigment
from whose delirium
the Arabs, the Jews, the Asians
the French, the English, the Americans
and the Africans all grow heads that keep expanding.

THE DIARY OF PEDRO DA CINTRA

Upon the hills of presentment
a rude wind releases cloudy roars
from the crucial preserves whose shadows
float and dance in the trembling waters,
a presidency upon my brows. Dark shadows
crouch in the canes of silver lightening
taming their views for a reticence
of their souls; their perched
thoughts moist in the alcove
of the gods. Quicksand of rugged threatening
seas lay mysterious before these simple
people running to embrace us from log-fires
between swollen dry stalks.

From the caves of the looming mountain
the solid world begins its growth
while upon my brow I feel the fallacy
in the theory of a once flat
earth. Thick clouds drop
like stars upon aghast animals
while my sedulous Portuguese eyes pierce
a prismatic rain for a book of green stones
to hunt the lions tails.

O lustrous gem you crash into pieces of stars
hiding from me the route to India and China
upon whose ghostly waves my limping
ship would dance with its cargo of an African
discovery; and what I now behold is a warrior
land in the meaning of a lion's roar—the verdure
of agelessness in a million palms.

I want to go into your virginity,
black mountains and confront the
burning eyes of your invisible
lions, which I shall take back home so that I may
be equal to Prince Henry. In this fifteenth
century I take a nautical plunge forcing myself
through the white mountains of Europe
with my call to be a navigator around
the world, ending in a lion's den.

O sea flowers open up the love of these locals
so that my sailing feet may not step
on their mercurial lanes as my voyage
of discovery in this year of our Lord
fourteen sixty-two begins on the paws of lions
crouching beneath my torment while
I christen Sierra Lyoa!

CHILD CHOOSES HIS PATH

A step waits to step into his step
the void inside of which a mustard seed
could grow to nurture and make a tall
tree out of him. He has heard mother talk
of it; he has heard father talk of it; he
knows mother is searching for the mustard
seed with spectacles in her eyes. She saw
it in an anthology of human
anatomy. His father asks him
to sow it in the soil but he chooses
to disperse it blindfolded. Only age ten
petiole of a man with a thousand ministering
unto his single step—other steps
willing to back his step. But he wants to live
without the indecorous fashion fig
trees combing whirlwinds in his sky; he wants
to wipe his sweat with a cloth and
not leaves. Sitting on a seaside rock,
he laughs at the oozing pus of the clan
as it rolls backward seeking
his lampshade; he is already
in the dunghill of the twentieth century shooting apexes
at the gravesite of the undead.

THE SIERRA LEONE I LOVE

Through the thorax of her peninsula I edge
starving waters; the flare of revolt recrudesce
in me as my country's blood seeks the asphodel—
the purity of verse in the alluvia of gravid skulls
where the moon long ago carved a heart for Freetown;
and now pouring milk, it embraces me with the haunches
of exaggerated hills. My country, running around

In circles lurching where the De Ruyter stands
like a stone, where the phoenix perches to compose
me the jazz a revolution of barrage. In this land
where the savannah is allotropic, my dreams
smash testicles in my belly with the rest of everything
coming against me like a desert to meet with the many
oases stored in green leaves of white eggs with blue insides.

In the core of my love my Sierra Leone
explodes, renting my resolve, my surreal poetry;
and so like the waters of the sea I starve in the corridor
of my dog days; my countrymen come in penumbral
shadows rocking oxymoronic overtures. The tree
under which I live sheds on me auburn leaves
each time I examine my agnail—bard/poet man-child.

Ebenezer Calendar brings forth the sphinx from
the hills and other high places to the road to combine
with the peninsular excreta of the wretched
countrymen. Presently I submit myself to my country
pedigree of those who have marched through Maphantha
stabling their hearts like philosophers seeking in many
beautiful phases the brother, the reptilian resting
its ancient jawbone on the icosahedrons; and I like
they want to write the centrifugal poem that would outlive
the rogue politicians of my country. I have dreamt
of building an ark to gather around me Sierra Leone's
unborn children to whom I shall read fluvial poetry of flowers

GIVE ME FREE!
for Sengbe Pieh

I must be ahead of dawn
to sweep the remaining dark of night,
and wash clean the thousand grains
in the moon. I have already strangled
the cocks and slaughtered their voices
in their throats with the help of Opo Wasaneh
who hang their cords in the dark forest.

A NEW PLANET

The drawl of sleep lingers in my yawn
corrupting night colors in my barricaded
orb; a lid-bridge conjured a planet,
the size of Saturn to embrace my cloudy
dreams. I am the creator of life forms
in the new planet; and from my reasoning
creatures breathe existence.

I do not think myself alien merely
because I have a big brain or because
there coils a restless thread of space without
the thick layers of planet earth. My orb
is seized by the common magnet with the thread
coiling unto itself mutable and productive.

At once I begin to wish my planet well
though its darkness is yet unclear
and its vast space unoccupied. My planet
runs into a rage. I contain it with my orb
so neatly closed, so neatly shut, away
from the anger of earth and other planets.

LETTER TO MY DAD

Dear Dad,

I'll never betray your trust in me even
as the tongue-taste wind narrows
my path-wish. The memory of Oscar Wilde's
poem of red war brightens my journey in the dark
tin-alleys. I no longer can move in time
with the legs you carved for me; and I no longer trust
bonfire songs since I discovered that heaven
too can outlive its essence with its
godliness. Yesterday its vast

Land covered the green Sunday foliage
peopled by robo-Neanderthals among whom I now
make my dwelling. You taught me to rope the Good book
to the wind but I now live in a place where
the gods have betrayed their own centuries
and the angels no longer fly about with birds
of the same feathers; a forest where lions stare
at the gods who dare to soften their manes when they no
longer can gnarl at the rainforests. When the leopard
licks the blood of its victims.

O Gethsemane, the immobile trees bleed in their roots.
You would think trees here will submit themselves
to man; but wait till I tell you about flowers
whose pollens are squeezed in dead cups for strange saints
coming alive in a new cathedral. These trees have breasts
to bosom a Golgotha. Their drums are not beaten
by blue ecology. Nectar-loving butterflies and scorpion
angels rattle in fig trees. Evenings no longer wait

At the door but in my veins. Their nerve-effrontery
is not credited to a god but iron. Here metal pity
has no tears in the eyes. Its venom is described
in many books that are bestsellers
in crowded markets. I come upon a temple
full of monks manufacturing gods whom they ask to pay
retribution for slavery. But father, there is one
god they quarrel over, the one to be made with invisible
materials. You are not yet dead but already I feel
orphaned. In this telescopic canal I am a man*scape*
unto myself. The graphs of life are carefully designed
in spider webs above the colors of embarrassed
tigers. Nothing is congealing in this landscape
of red war. I carry the memory of monkeys
springing for locusts, and falling down with glaucoma,
and of a pride coming upon their mangy
frames. But I have made a nocturnal

Promise lost in my breasts, so I eat the bile of a sick
goat to trace it; but I'm ready to bring it to you
in verses of baboons beating their breasts over
lighted candles. To them the wax is a moon god who sleeps
in their deathbeds. I discover father that the snake
is an apple tree by night and by day it searches

For a thorax to glide the world. My sockets are now
empty like archaeological texts. I discover a bat's Braille
in a giant tree. On the marbles of its speech I trace
a patchwork. I have discovered that in the company
of the blind the Braille is noisy. The demand
of its consonants burdens its vowels. And I must
sooth my palms on the little balls of the Braille

From these strange clouds. Tonight I am awakened
by rabid dogs who were once beautiful poppies
on the shore my virgin sister stretched. They brandish
the same teeth I once shaped with shells; they wag
their tails once lost between their legs; they come against
me in my yellow whirlwind as my palms bleed
on the blind Braille's sharp consonants. I take solace
in the shore recalling the virgin sisters,
and I can see the big muscles of the sea approaching
me; the forgotten innocence of the dogs
In their laughter. What do I call the empire

Built in Redheart Land? Maybe a thirst of fire
in dinosaurian window skull illuminating the man Adam
who failed to walk the earth. I admire the orange
yellow fear at conference tables, the white lips
at labor camps, and jungle roads, the grassman
overflowing the green silence, the indefatigable animal
breeding the extinct barbarian, the growth of the foetus
inside the fragile egg, and the *boom* of a bang
already bigger than theory. Father, a promise
is a promise, and I'll keep moving on.

Your son

LATE LAST NIGHT

prominent figures rose from
my thirst. I saw fingers
like vistas grabbing
stars wherever the clouds

withdrew. In my clan
flowers have taken
their tolls negotiating
laughter in the curve;
visions assumed lenses
in these beds where

seeds were watered
to rot. On rising from
the thirst these figures
of speech hunger for the desert
floating through…

through the impenetrable sand
as the new day, cracked out of a nightingale egg
sheds upon a mind in growth.

OBLATION

My Sierra Leone I embrace you
in desperation with my flower screaming
between my fingers. I've held it these several
seasons refusing it access to form a shadow
of its own. How can I be so cruel as to give
you a flower that has negotiated a shadow
with the sun? You have always protected me
with your hurricane rocks and restless waters.

I went out and got you this flower in the field
while the dead eyes of my brothers wept; and I fought
and killed the mangy dogs which have been fattened
by the flesh; and when I was done, I killed
the memories which opened a battle
field in me. I can safely say my Sierra Leone that I'm
your prisoner, and I go into you holding
my flower against the wind.

EVERYMAN A JOURNEY

My breath is red with pain
burning the thread of a thousand
glowing wax. I am in a desert pressed
hard by mortal hooves. A desert that has learnt
to lick its pain with its wet tongue. My grandfather had
stopped
by to drink of its tears, not the waters
of its oases—he headed straight
to hell where he met poets shaping
unknown heavens in Roman numerals with
borrowed calligraphy. When my father took it he knew
it was a road less travelled. He was on it on horse
back knocking down discriminating woods,
erecting periods on crossroads where most peninsulas
began their circulars around dark rocks that were bent
on meeting the sky hunch after hunch. I do not wish
to dwell in the desert. Like those before me
I only want to be left alone
to make my journey between heaven & Hell.

IN THE MIDDLE OF MY JOURNEY, I PAUSE

The naked white star
has fallen into the calabash,
and the water inside has turned black.
The star incapable of reverberating
sinks to the bottom,
clothed in its whiteness, and

I go dipping my body into it fingerward; I immerse
into the black water mouthing my name, seeking
the roots of my birth in the fragmented
star glittering in the woods. In the water, I'm making
my change,
pushing deep-ward
dipping forward,
journeying into the womb of my past –

—the womb—the past.
The mother who sipped the water of my father saw
the white star in my eyes the moment

I was born. She cried laughing; she laughed crying,
thinking of the years to come, when
her son shall drink of the first blood.

I am in the middle of my journey!

I shall take a man to give me
a wife, a wife to give me a son, a son to give me
a man. This shall come to pass in my salt-water days,
or so I dream in exile. My fire like a new rainbow
cannot be reflected in the calabash. Reflected are

Those who flattered me through
And through, beginning with my father who
Whitewashed me in my mother's hands.

WINDOWS ARE A PRIVATE THING

Move cursor
shift fender
enter super highway

Figures rise in thirst,
from the void of weak torrent—
monologue—
chalk to write the surface
of seabreath caught ashore;
Harmattan lived and lost—
eyes change dresses.

"My window is bigger than yours!"

Match–flare check—
neighbors' white fangs brighten
the night with flashes of hearts.

Magnet minds,
Windowphobia! That is my heartbeat
in verse;
windowpane

Move cursor
shift fender
close windows

155

SINGING AS A POET

I creep into the alcove
of woes, guarded by firefly of hunger
and torment listening to the whispering
wind on the dry leaves
swaying back and forth with a genesis
for my song . I have become a ubiquitous
poet, smashing the interplanetary
mirror, carving each jointed bit like
a cartographer with a colonialist's
mind, a snail in my eaves or a sniffing dog
breaking the mouths of radios
whose unwritten odes I sing.
I hide in the king's court with little interest
in the courtiers executive voices
or in the hypocrisy of poetless
bards, but like the glass of wine I cling
until the clincher, then I discover
songs to write and sing,
metaphors mixed or unmixed
in my possession,
history safe for posterity—
more significantly an executive
voice to say aloud
after comparing the gold of kings
to the sliver in the surface of the sea, "Damn
To royal highnesses!"

TRIAL

A teardrop
is memory
circulating
the relative torment.
The image
at the curve of my life
is the vacuum into which
forlorn dreams abandon
a man like me
and here
where my diction
grows into a poem.
I have claimed
to be watchful of illegal
shadows
which themselves
suffer the glow
of evening moons.
Would you laugh
at me if I offered
myself a certificate
of merit after
I have failed
to be a stream
on the left side

of the river without of course
dreaming to be any on the right
side? Don't mock
me. I know why others,
And not you who now
read me would
gnash their teeth in
rage. You suffer a decided
hunger as you laze around
the point I am going to nail here
at the end of this sentence.

VENOM

When red blood cells
swell like deformed nodes
the tree in the inside of a man
eclipses the moon and the branches
clear the skies of its slow traffic

Then on the outside
sweating under his cabinet everything suddenly
smells raw with mahogany.

His system, charging malaria,
announces a conflict
between his inside and outside
and as blood and skin
taste of each other's salt
the real carnivore takes a drive.

He has a way to assume
the shape of a mountain
whiles he maintains unkempt
images under famished stars.

MEMORIES OF HOME WHILE HOME IN EXILE

I have memories of how Sierra Leone
looked in the days of …in the category
of yesterday's history; her fjord discharging
painful pus—being that it was fibrous of my
countrymen's labyrinthine joint it was fitful in uterus
suffocating as storm in calabash
taking from, shaping through pergolas. I have…and
it is related to my now terra–cotta roots,
that world that died in obscurity
unfolding the images of its skeletal scroll
revealing itself like fingers jutting into dream;
that world which emptied itself into oases
measured my courage inside its peninsula,
as I went through it—desert supporting
desert like a castaway.

Today as I journey through America these memories
come to me as hills of temper; sometimes
in multitudes of leaves charging through chasms
down to the ethos of my reptilian age lingering as a
shadow near the many battlefields in which I was
Killed a thousand times but did not die.

ON BEING ASKED TO WRITE A POEM FOR MY COUNTRY

Secretpains
secretpains
secretpains
secretpains
secretpains
secretpains
Secretpains
secretpains
secretpains
secretpains
secretpains
secretpains
secretpains
Secretpains
secretpains
secretpains
secretpains
secretpains
secretpains
secretpains
Secretpains
secretpains
secretpains
secretpains
secretpains

secretpains
secretpains
Secretpains
secretpains
secretpains
secretpains
secretpains
secretpains
secretpains
Secretpains
secretpains
secretpains
secretpains
secretpains
secretpains
secretpains
Secretpains

THE SONG OF SIA LEONA

Singing the Birth

THE PARABLE OF THE SEED

Gem phlegm

Poured as the vomit of the rainbow
and from within its prism emerged
the head of Sia Leona wrapped in cloying
leaves, deeply buried in sprouted warmth
where spiritual colors hypnotized her eyes.

Reactionary

Sperm mingled with blood
as the invisible cudgel
of the angels of pain
pulled her forth by the hair,
greasing her through the ligature
which from century
to century has returned
the rib to the ribcage.
Her nervy
hair of fine epidermal cells
grew out of virginity and

spun, overflowing green
calabashes and as she
hiccupped at the first touch
of water, the river surged
into the hills.

Her hair

Came breathing,
hurrying into the world,
assuming the shape of
skyleaves as the packed
follicles spread out to fill
the emptiness of space
fattening and full of light.

She emerged

In her wholeness,
increasing in size and volume,
possessing the edges
everywhere God erected a border
with darker circular pigments
showing divine marks on her skin,
her body the womb gave up.

As a babe

She suffered the push that brought
her forth as a woman–child; suffered
the tension on her edges

when she emerged to fit
the ancestral cloak, assuming
the shape of a tree in a world
overrun by carbon dioxide.

Earth darkened

To accommodate her florescence
as mirth berthed in palms of longing;
and with the beryllium–blue
hope dawned as light.

HER WORLD

Merged with the world
as she subdued her ankles
and limbs to the control
of the branches of unseen trees
that wedged her soul
into the cosmos.

Should she have

Eaten her afterbirth or returned cold
the blood her mother wasted?
or tangled her intestines with her hair
or kicked passed her cautious push

The midwives

Lost their fingers in her heir,
returning home leprous,
possessed by the spirit
of the afterbirth.

Her birthday

Wrapped up with her
birthright, opening up
and pushing back her puberty
with combined muscles
as many gathered
around demanding blind old
age to open the riddle
rattling before their eyes.

She cried

Advancing starlight-like. Crying
several times reporting
her appearance in the world
in tattoos of comets, floating
like the ark, surviving
a measureless flooding.

From the river

She rose,
laying her startling hair
on current waves like lighting
hidden in the trees and threading
across the sky to catch
a glimpse of the world.

Drums

In the alcoves of the hills
complemented voices on high, and
the strangled necks of the sacrificial
lambs splattered blood on her
hair to make it shine like power.

The criers

With legs as swift as a horse's
crushed against ancestral
power, seeking a free bid to report
the fulfillment of a new tabula rasa,
crouching on empty grips, flying
with an open scroll wedging
among scribes in this outcry.

Singing the Miracle

OF CABBAGES AND QUEENS

That night

Four wise goats,
drunk with
the milk of the moon
and possessed with –

Gold –
Diamonds-
Frankincense-
Myrrh-
hastened
from the east, west, north
and south. One from the hills

another from across the sea,
yet another from above the sky
another from beneath the ground
pulled by the electrifying
follicles of Sia Leona,
chewing the cud,
chewing upon that. The vast
meadows beheld their idols
against a wind
of no rhythmic poesy; itself dancing
to the resonance of dry leaves
and a faint drumming
from young morocco. They tried
to talk to each other,
but they soon discovered that
they couldn't,
not even to name
the child they were to name
the child they were off to adore; but they
remembered the words taught to anyone
counting himself a discoverer:

and on that day
a strong wing whirled
exactly where the earth breathes;
a prismatic dust formed

in the likeness of an image in a mirror
and at sundown a Pedro cried, 'Eureka!'

This was the crisping habit
that led them to Sia Leone;
into a landscape busy
forming itself. They got tangled
in the desert labyrinth where
evening neon distorted their faces
on the bright side of light; and
with all their might they leapt
into the invisible ropes of high,
their bottoms rising above their heads
kicking their hinds into the follicles
of space. Under the thatched
roof of her birthplace
the first goat offered her a cyst
and opened up a prism of rainbow
inside her so that she too became
a bringer of rainbows; and unto it
was added the surpluses of heaven's
footstool so that she became a promise;
the second goat offered her a scroll
holding the November moon above it for long,
reflected into a baptismal blue of water;
the third goat offered her the green

leaves of the virgin sin, each of which ran
with blades from the apex down;
and the fourth goat took all the gifts
from her, planting in her eyes a burning star.

Back in the shanties

Sia Leone's folks still flabbergasted,
followed in their hounds-tooth check,
in the disturbing eclogue of their heartbeats
in solitary labyrinth
they pounded their souls
panting in constriction
speaking voices to the firmaments.

That night

Their freshness
corrugated into exhaustion
lifting them above their myopic egos
which were long spread on their zinc
breeding societal rebirth of rust, and
blotting every sign of being a
people alive. But following the arrival
of Sia Leone night hung its heavy hand

171

on the mothers and on those
who vigil-led the living
souls of the monotonous hunger
sipped as saliva
down the horizon of echoes
sounding staccato beats inside
their vacant concaves. At day break
while Sia Leona slept,
they gulped the excessive sun
and loomed over its china as
it shattered in the sea.

You have heard it said

That Sia Leona was the lost Pleiad
born into distant palms, but I tell
you, this child got conceived
in imageless spirits that descended
on rainforest virgins; that she carried a mountain
amid the argument she also carried a sea;
the perception that she nurtured lions in her breasts
giving her a forever calabash embrace;
that she was the scorching sun
plagued with the thirst of Siddhartha,
condemned to plenteous love
designed into starlight follicles

172

wasted upon her like an olive oil. But Sia Leona
is not a woman of the ribs. She came
as a river that broke the neck of ocean
by the creek, and as a peninsula
possessing a vast array.

Secretpain is a woman

Blending with the pain of Sia Leone's
in a darksome virginal forest. Her hair filled
the corners of the three firestones
where the midwives
buried her umbilical cord. Sia Leona
like all infants was unable to bear witness
to what she saw even as her blood
bank was held in strings ready
for the bridge of transition. The bittersweet
apple in her passage—double-edged agony,
promiscuity—the burden
of thirst and want. Awaking in the blood
of the clan she spiralled like a serpent
toward those who wished to become
true women bearing that harvesting
the apple was a sectorial
ideal. She suddenly mastered
the magical art of survival.

Sia Leona

Lived her life
shadow and shade,
Avoiding the beam of the light. The drifting
days brought splendor
into her ethos.   Each evening as her
fingers played the idiophones on her head,
the desert blades of the Sahara
sharpened their edges on her hair,
and sea navigators
drifted by the ocean wind
are knitted by the dribbling
follicles of Sia Leona
laid her hair on her breasts and roared
like the lions inside of her; and floating
on the sea, she emerged ageless
like a stone, spreading her power
like shards of rays. The maids
lowering their calabashes scooped
the excesses of her hair, wishing to stick
each follicle to theirs like
the sunrays on the water-rays.

Singing Anguish

AN INSIDE OBSESSED WITH RAINBOWS

First Sia Leona preferred

A creation of her own world
where no principality stringed to her dream;
any azure clinging to her palms
shattered in stars; and as she soared
above the dark woods her flight like that of a bird
became real. A mat appeared
under her and a throng emerged
from her hair. Gray shards encircled
her netting a thick clouds on her image,
dripping with oil, ripping from her dark skin
the veil of time, scribbled in bygone
centuries. A hypnotic star
twinkled at her, making her eyes lose
their water –lights and at once
she perceived her color
departing her skin. Her hair tangled
on star-strings, and from the foreground distance
short a finger-like blade. Sia Leona in tears
tore her dark colored clothes. From the rainbow
she spat fire at the hidden blades of the green
leaves but the jaws of the blade tore it like
the early moments of a divided kingdom

whose two halves tumbled out of guided
routes. The blades advanced creating
a shrilling sound of thirst, tearing
into her. They tore with hunger
as she cried in anger
and the strings released her hair and the dark
bundle fell off her feet
as a dark laughter tore across
the woods with an undying echo
perching on the wings of time.

Fear cut across her twenty-first century

Gnawing at her in communal
tones. Latent blisters possessed her
like a detonating lightning
creating a world in her world,
the phantom of being—scared! And like the fallen
breasts of an exhausted mother her rocks
gave way and a whole vision collapsed
and her stem of hope
tear-danced on blades wrecking
her range in her tempered hills;
alcoves ran extended windows of impediments
in the ethos of her loam—the prop

Of her dark pride. She laid her legs
On the quiet ground of her neighbors who
Like her were long left in the nude
under the scrambled roots of withering
trees whose seeds drifted ashore
driven mad by the battered
looks of these prismatic bodies. The red breath
of daggers prompted wreaths at her doorstep
sounding dirges of the unachieved
centuries. Her heart burst
out of the webbed thatch of her past
as her rivers down the city of Freetown
drowned into the lazy ocean,
uttering concertos of cavalcades
of follicles and blood suffocated inside
the breath of time. The seasons
confused her memory, shaping it first
as a sun and then as a moon. Since then she
began screaming into nights
whenever fire yelped
in her. After the strangers had
left in the wake of her madness
Sia Leona founded a mirror that captured her misery.

She sat by the bank of the river

With an unintelligible song on her lips
She combed the mutated strands
of her hair. The asthmatic
Wind buried its breath in, digging
into the forest of her head. This is the same river
her hair shuttled through as a terrestrial
being—the nature of her soul, the sapphire,
gem blue. In those days when the rustling wind
fanned the dark materials of her continent,
when the bard's flute sang to the breath
of her breasts she would throw her pillars
into the sky. In those days
wild plants strangled
the necks of voiceless birds
that bestrode the nest
of her nightingale. In those days she
flung her head to the corners of the earth
reciting the hendecasyllabic verses
of the rainbows inside of her,
embracing the waves
that created the web
to consume her flesh and return
her as a concept. But soon after that
the asthmatic wind slipped

into her and in the heavy leaden time
her neck, humbled by the power
of her head
–collapsed!

Her hair
completely washed off river,
gathered on a hunched rock, O epidermal
cells! When it crawled back, it was thick and sticky
with the smell of fever possessing each follicle.

After the follicles

Had withered,
after the cells
too had mutated,
and when the strands
no longer stretched
they gathered on the hunch
of a rock. When its prism no longer
connected to the florescence
of the forests from which her cord
had long been severed,
a battered dawn fell.

Her hair then parted
many paths with the strands
withdrawing into themselves, forming
four big mops with cardinal
stems which themselves were
divided into many
halves, each flailing
to the wind. After the spell
had vanished like
an anaesthetic, her hair
grew eight more mops. As she reached
her hands to feel them, they changed
into heads, screaming hard to detach
themselves from her heard. Sia Leona
was flung onto the ground by the screaming
heads; and in her madness she reached
for a Damoclean sword tasting
the blood of the blood of the bled.

Laying her sword she wept
knowing that her valley
was closing in on her;
she knew that her rainbows
were fading inside and washing
Into the river. She dragged her tired
feet to the foot of the mountain,

seeking a double pergola
and a cave to surrender her grief.

Echoes swelled in her flesh,
in her thews were
lachrymal pus. Her people
from whose mouths once flowed
the doxology of her true name
and the peacock of her image
had betrayed her! These heads,
these mops were due to be severed!

MY IMMIGRANT BLOOD

STRANGE FRUIT*

with my scapulars sewn wild, I spring
from my own pedestrian egg
among avocadoes and pawpaws,
mangoes and oranges,
bananas, pineapples, and strawberries—
and far from being dead, I hang
on the heartbeats
that keep me still. Breaking
blood in meditation while guerrillas
lynch me as a bloodclot. But I drip in lodes
feeding lungs. I drip in lodes filling
saproots. I drip in lodes pushing time, and
my fragrance circulates the earth. Ripe in
the inside and raw on the outside
I'm in a state *I* only know
as the permanence of pain,
even as I hang from this tree,
dangling

*inspired by a poem of the same title written by Lewis Allan, a Jewish
lyricist. The song first recorded by Billie Holiday*

MY RESPONSIBILITIES AS A PEOPLE'S POET

The games are over, and
I return to report the wars; the night

is the excreta of the day, and
I return to report the smell; the man

is the child of the sun, and
I return to report the scorch; the rain

is the water of the seas, and
I return to report the flood; the bridge

is the secret of death, and
I return to reverse the clock; the road

is the hunger of the mind, and
I return to fence the graveyard; the graveyard

is the house of the unborn, and
I return to donate some blood; the second

is the brother of the minute, and
I return to alert the hour; the edge

is the end of the mind, and
I return to caution the philosopher; the philosopher

is the angel of death, and
I return to alert the living; the flower
is the gun of the lover, and
I return to reason with the heart; the truth

is the sword of the lie, and
I return to arm the victim; the lie

is the smile of the truth, and
I return to trap the perpetrator; the victim

is the brother of the perpetrator, and
I return to clean the blood; the wretched

is the child of the affluent, and
I return to the science of humanity; the subject

is the reverse of the object, and
I return to bury my double edged sword; the dead

is the audience of the living, and
I return to act the drama; the living man

is the judge of the dead, and
I return to argue their case; the forest

is the infant of the jungle, and
I return to study the law.

CONFLUENCE OF HANDS

I open a conference in my throat
to discuss my singular diversity. During the
plenary, I shuttle to the ends of the earth
to consult with aboriginal chroniclers regarding
the history of the people of the posthumous race
who departed the Garden chained or chainless.
I lecture mainly on DNA, of the pedestrian self
and the rainbow effect in every mortal's blood
dripping on skeletal bones in the laboratory of God.
The past has covered too many miles,
advancing evidence of my evidence;
and the new conclusion is that I have continued
to evolve as the same species. But who
the hell declared me a Darwinian fossil
in a single specimen of my many selves?

THE DESERT SPEAKS OF BODY BAGS

for the helpless Sudanese Children
dying in Dafur

O excruciating desert!

I am that polio child in your belly,
the one you have prepared a place
for on your back;

I come forth with a nauseating mind
I shall be born the day the sun bursts into flames.

For now I fill your heart noon after noon,
and I feel my heels cracking the sands of your sea.

After I am born, do not grow tired of seeing
the river coming down my face.

I cry for myself thinking
about the thousand Arabian and African nights
full of body bags the burden I shall inherit from you,
night of the fireflies and of the Harmattan!

THE LONG WALK TO MOTHERLAND

Even after my cousins have buried
her, I think my mother won't die.
Yesterday, in exile I covered her
with the brown skin
of my grandmother.

My mother should not be covered
by some cold hands and
with some strange earth
to envelop her body.

If I had covered her with the first dirt,
our two hearts would have rested in peace.

In exile, I do not know when the mails
will leave, but I hope to see
this invocation posted to wherever she is.

THE COTTON TREE CRIES OF THIRST

The sun that journeys across this desert
throws a heavy force of weight on me.
Many a morning I wake up thirsty to my roots,
and I go blindly searching for a drink.

I may have a heavy weight,
but I look out for myself and others;
they call me the Cotton Tree Man
squatting in the square;
and when the day beats my head with its rattan,
I run the risk of a bad night left behind by the sun.

A kiss of night without a twinkling star!

When my branches scrape the sky,
they search the sea, the hills, and the peninsula
for the treacherous stranger lost in my shadow,
for the native son who is quick to fart into my dry lungs;
they make me thirst, they itch my throat with pain.

I dig with my roots deep into the earth seeking
routes when hunger calls me all kinds of names.
I shoot into cold soils and hot soils,
forgetting which one is the heaven and which one
the hell; but I am very determined to go beyond them
to look for that which quenches my thirst.

I DREAM OF AFRICA

and let my brothers know I walk the streets of exile
clutching their bullets in my soul!

                                        Syl Cheney-Coker

I need the slumber of an ant
and not that of an elephant which drops
its body to the ground once a year to sleep
dead and deep. I dream of Africa

In exile, of Africa within me; a continent within
a continent. It is this I dream of in the slumber
of an ant, a simple dream and a simple yearning.
I go through the eye of a needle

Like a thread, following my dream into the river
where, instead of drowning, I float above to hold a conference
with little tiny fishes who unlike the elephant, but like the ant
do not grow tired, and now tell me how to push my world
     ahead

Of me. "Go on dreamer," the fishes
say, "but, you don't sleep like the elephant,
for one thing, you do not have its size, which
makes it able to fight even when asleep."

But it is the hour I want to talk about, the hour
within the minute, when the three hands of the clock
go on striking aloud in the graveyard; the second
beating against the minute, against the hour at

Twelve, three, six, and nine, and at twelve again,
and still the graveyard would not breathe because time
is the only one left alive after the flood of theories
have ransacked the veins of Africa. This continent

In the far south is in my ant head. I drink painkillers
tonight to work on my head because I carry in me
the advice of fishes not to trust my lungs to the wind,
especially when the wind is suffocated with the smell

Of the hawk who is known to sail on its wings quietly
like the steps of a shadow in the light of a 2000 watts
bulb. A continent staggers in my head along a road
of appetites, of more than three colored traffic

Lights, and with indecipherable road signs displayed
in the faces of the used moons of the world; and I know
I'm on the road to embrace you mother, singing
that song you always hummed under your bare breath!

MY SISTER, THARA

I love you, beautiful woman,
but my imagination mutilates your face
because of what I saw happen to my sister.
She had wild dimples but
the horse wore its hooves into them
building a rough house with rough thatch.
The black wild fronds of her head
dragged all the mountains across the land
to rest them upon our dead father's testicles.
Perched between the two tight grips of a bar,
the bastard uprooted the cotton tree
from my sister's guts. You should see the roots
with their bleeding fingers starving for breath.
You should see the six foot, five inch
lizard that ran down my sister's thighs
when the bastard came upon her.
How much passion do you think an Alsatian dog
has to rape its kind in a crowded street?
Well, I'm telling you about a man who swallowed
all of earth's air and still controlled the gravitational force
to dig up the fresh corpse of my sister's unborn babe.

I love you, beautiful woman,
and I see my sister in you as she was before
the storm. Her name was Thara.

Every morning she opened her teeth to the sky
to brighten the sun; and in the night she perched
her eyes among the stars.
Whenever her tooth ached and she wanted to be left alone,
the sky threatened the night
until Thara exposed her teeth in her sleep till morning.
At daybreak,
the rain fell at her feet
to wash the stubborn mud cloying for warmth.
That was my sister before the storm.

I love you, beautiful woman,
but I hate the tiny shapes of memory
coming to me as fireflies
in the deep stillness of my gaze
because those shapes are not a reality.
Reality is when the soul dies in the shoe
because it is mortal; the shadow scraping
its nothingness against objects with a rattling silence.

When the storm came beating rattan on my head
I coughed blood, coughing it red on my white
robe, coughing it down my feet
for Thara, the sister who once fed me the milky
stars in the night sky where I now behold
her bright face the bulbous of firmaments.

ALONG THIS AVENUE WHERE I LIVE

When the tormented soul is stabbed
countless times, the body is put right!

I hope to buy a bottle of beer and
drink this woman further down my belly
and leave the rest to my factory workers.
That done, I shall turn my mind
to the thieves roaming my streets of exile,
and invite the beggars among them to dine
with me on my jewellery table.

Once when I was drunk I learned that when
you save the soul from destruction, the body dies
obeying with shame. It is this reason that a woman
crushed within me loses her soul to mine. The sperm
of my soul shall have some eggs to feast on then!

This world is so complex that every heartbeat
is an exclamation, and I wonder why people don't drop
dead more often than they now do. Yesterday
this woman came to me with a bandana desire,
to be the *she*-Christ rescuing my dying heart,
but who needs a woman and poetry in the same
soul when one is the heel the other the snake head?

Disproportionate my impossible fraxinella of soul,
indecomposable my hunger my many apples of exile,
and this long street with one dead end, and an insecure outlet
shall traffic a heavy cargo dumped in the middle of my heart!

The sheriff warned me to inscribe, "Oversized" on a cargo
going down the dead end of the avenue.
This mouth of mine is giving away my heart to the cops!
Shut up! Home the green bottles and keep busy
being a drunkard on the municipal avenue tax free!

Country of my cargo, where do I keep you
while I intoxicate a moment?
Mindful of the bozos tormenting your
belly, I might hire goliathan men to keep watch over
you on the lane off of the avenue that winds into my soul.

I go now to be with other drunkards but I shall return to be
your child, full only of your own opium fed me in childhood
farms where I first learned how to say 'Proud to be African!"
The music down the avenue has gone bad, and Sinatra
will not come into my soul bringing a violin.
I have no scriptures prepared for tonight;
how am I going to welcome these American birds
who have come to name this avenue after me?

THE MIDDLE PASSAGE

It is no longer a matter of time as the village mothers used
to believe it; no longer a wedding of waiting thoughts. Palm oil
has spilled over the earthenware as the infants willed it.
And all there is to do is to call the skilful gatherers who
have never jumped over a fallen mortar or pestle to wash
the soiled shrouds of the guardians. O for the bondless
innocence of the oil spillers to the silence of the village.
The forerunners are across the stream, and the waters
have gone too high in the middle. The frequent
waves bring us no clue about our own; they only stretch
inland to empty our barns. It is no longer a matter of time
as the village mothers used to believe it; no longer a wedding
of waiting thoughts. The forerunners should never have
been carted away in the first place.

O MOTHER

in the African November of 1965
earth path cleared
bull horns of the dead and the living
guarded post
sun-still day
my arrival
green leaves swayed
in their chlorophylls
yellow leaves of weak strength
fell lightweight to make space
mama pushed and pushed
the day contorted
she grinned
stiletto wind pierced her skin
death lingered
coiling around
the impatient hours
rain on roof thatch
quenching fire
landscape of waiters
from the idle ground
to the loaded soil
huts peopled to capacity
packed in the cocoa farm
children pushed their world

forward and brightly so
holding nothing back
nothing sacred
aiming to pull the new hand
to the playground
adults on benches
breastbeating the unhurt skin
children undermining and
tickling the dry wind with games
and all the while November
was rolling its belly
on the palm of the wind
and the wind was galloping in the air
and the air was aiming at the wind's head
with its *crocodilic* jaws
behind the shadow of the sky
and the sky was traversing the firmament
and the firmament was whispering to the river
and the river was flowing hard against the rock
and the river and the rock were arguing
about who between them was blind
but they were also arguing who between
them was holding back time
and all throughout
these whispers
these struggles
mama pushed

THE BUSINESS OF WAR

Was not known until I was shot
in the movie that had so been advertised
the clock dropped rolling over and over missing its own time
another mortar
the grandfather rose holding his head and screaming
those who knew the business plan slept
the dead were not part of their joint venture
the grandfather knew, no questions asked
the next mortar
cut his face into two, and he dropped and slept again
this time was for two hundred years until the final conflict
another mortar
the wedding of my sister, three unfinished years resumed
the couple went to the confession
the choir filled the vacuum and the audience
slept waiting for serious entrepreneurs
who would shout the halleluiah and release
the fornicators to speak in the pulpit or thereafter hold their
breath; another mortar
and the shovels bruised the belly of the soil
the business was taking shape
the sacrifices were burning in the open field
and the commanders were drinking palm wine
the air was filled with command and god nearly choked
in his corner videoing the duel that left him with

a mutilated tongue and lost for a miracle
the angels were not told to analyze
so the whole affair went on in the quietest of atmosphere
the clouds were busy suppressing their laughter
and when they could hold it no longer they gave up the ghost
the cannon turned on them and they too dropped shedding tears
the business was booming and all the while
doctors helped pregnant women
to supply fieldmen and fieldwomen
who marched like Neanderthals
some, so much in a hurry dragged along their umbilical
cords until someone told them
that once born to this earth, the umbilical chord
had to be chewed off
these fieldmen and fieldwomen
were quick to disappear into the dust
smart and vigorous on the ground
but very quick to find their way back into the warmth
where they first separated their bodies from their souls
another mortar
and the grandfather scared troubled by the sorrowful legs
of the premature men and women
his half face couldn't see enough of the big picture
for instance he knew nothing about the commanders
who had departed, and so he returned
to finish his two hundred years of sleep

another mortar
sounded again before I went into the middle
of the field to talk to the strange
men who said they were there to take over.

NIGHT IN GOLGOTHA

In Golgotha, darkness
emerges from undersea and
rests on the thighs of the sun
and very suddenly the stars
burrow into the sky and
disappear; and from those holes
gray dust spews.

I do not have what it takes
to martyr the flesh in this
corporate landscape.

I speak of agony in business
terms, and I open the cemetery
of my heart, searching for the
one skull who knows it all.

DIARY OF AN IMPRISONED JOURNALIST
For Paul Kamara, a fearless journalist

Two knives are broaching my heart
Two dogs peep out of my eyes and bark
I close the incisors, and my blood
Returns to the flesh, and my flesh
Returns to Maphantha prisons and to Pademba prisons
The jailers have not learned anything new
Not even that the smell of the prisons
Has become stronger. I'm worried
Watching these jailers running to the
Honeycomb, leaving only
Their shadows to guard the prisoners.
Yesterday you asked
Me to write and tell you all about
The family farm, but I notice that
You are too scared to read my letter
In the face of the sun. Remember I told
You I'm prepared to die because
I'm ashamed to confront my children
And not able to say to them that once
A thief was set free and made a leader
In the land! Tonight I sit in the dark
Listening to the rattling bones of my
Countrymen who died because they SPOKE!
I'm the coelacanthine brother
Living the bitter peninsula

204

O Mountain! O Sea!
Like you I crouch in my prison
Having surrendered all my hours

And my wristwatch on the left hand to those who know
How to say, "Kill him for his bad verses!"
Yesterday the judge ordered me silenced
For attempting to be a historian
"It is not meet that a journalist
Becomes a historian," he barked.
At that hour, the two dogs peeped
Out of my eyes and barked too.
By the time you read this diary
The beloved country shall no longer have a past
I shall die here, the jailers off to the honeycomb
Told me; and I can hear the rogue politicians
In the mahogany night screaming,
"Burn all those books at the gates of Eden!"
You and I know history is graffiti.
Don't cry for me if I die in the shadow of the moon
Particularly so that I know your heart is heavy
With the grief of hearing about
The Mabayla massacre, that poor community
Sinking below the Rokel river. It is for this same reason
I will not remind you of the street named in honor
Of Sani Abacha where I saw hundreds of youth
dying between the soldier and the politician.

205

THE CHAIN

In the beginning there wasn't a chain
Until that first ahoy that shook the reeds of the tides
And then a ship berthed and threw
Out a dirty line which caught my siblings by the ankles
Pulling them to the depth of the sea.

I listened to the dragging noise of the chain
Crushing a hammer to their heads
And like a fish in the tremor of foreign hunger
My siblings waded in the current.

I hid behind the bulrushes and other stems of hope
Listening to the wailing of my siblings
As their bodies merged with the hiccup of the sea
And the waters belching after a long hunger.

The chain tangled them choking their throats
Dragging them on its rough back
Across three centuries of my torment.

Many years later I threw myself into the mouth of the crocodile
And discovered my long lost siblings at the
End of the century's digestive process.

TRAP

And so I tell my story
of how one day I came closer to death.
But like you, I soon forgot how
that death was a hungry lion
who ate my flesh down to my abdomen
before I fixed the bones of my legs
and fled;

or

how it was the story of a whore,
and after stretching her,
paid her money, I shot her
nudity with my eyes—and she,
plucking out my sockets, reached for the camera
of my retinas to extract her photos; and
I was only too lucky to pluck some stars
from the sky that helped me get away;

or

how after the beers I'd drunk
formed a sea in my belly, a tiny little
fish began eating my intestines,
beginning with the larger one,

eating it with such patience as would
a god of pain. I quickly strangled
it with the smaller intestine and
drowned it in the water before
I breathed a sigh of relief;

or

how on election day, I voted the noisiest
candidate and his displaced philosophy
to the seat of representation; and even
when booed I carried him on my backbone.
I would not allow him to fall. I became the slave
of his burden. And when he was properly seated,
he crushed a hammer to my skull. Thank goodness
for an angel who gave me spare parts wrought out
of him the day he was toppled.
I was able to patch up my head;

or

how a rat teased me into a race
round and round my head, round and
round my idleness, half way round my village,
then half way round the big city;
its four legs becoming eight, and I could not

multiply myself. I cried for the brother of me
by me; I pondered at my human sorrow as the rat
boasted sixteen legs. I bent and crouched on four,
becoming the man, the beast, the humanimal;
the rat was still swifter.

AFTER THIS VITUPERATION
The last hymn of Ken Saro-Wiwa and other immortals

*"El Placer de sufrir, de odiar, me tine
la garganta con plasticos venenos."*
--Cesar Vallejo

I am that broken woman from the old
road on her way to the new grave. Having
burnt my suns with immense energy
and my legs tricked by the stubborn wax,
I have to move on. Yesterday the moon

Was good to me, but I found her too dull
for company; and now that I long for her,
she hangs over her desert lingering
in her own sorrow brought about by the very
clock beating over my head. To what

Divinity shall I sing my night songs
when the new gongs are waiting
for the petals of a new magic – O Mars!
O Earth! seizing me by my hands, you lead
me to your Golgotha, but I'm certain to leave behind

My footmarks, so that when I return as
the subterranean immortal to massacre your souls,

what would be your dreams of mating shall not
anymore produce planets in the fathomless

Memory of your orbit. Let my heart of withering
flesh embrace this Waterloo that must tame
this intolerant mind of mine. Remember that I shall have
the reverse pleasure of shattering your guitar strings
and silencing your birds in the throat, crowding your

Heads. O for the old savannah shoe and its metacarpal
master, the faithful garment caving the ribs,
the dried up tooth, the broken jaw,
the skull and its fragments, I shall hope for
the key to trap your impossible Medusas. My heart

Gladdens at the prospect of achieving life, man being
guano for man! Let my newness twist the minds
of your firmaments. Between my tired
bones and this agony you have
made me, I shall be drunk with the kef

brewing in my heart. Go ahead! Open up and
burst the belly of your igneous rocks and scorch my skin;
kill the children of the noon and cast boils on
the infants of the night; beat the clock faster
above me and speed my departure.

211

MY AUTOBIOGRAPHY IN FIFTY LINES

I'm a poet; fuse with words to achieve immortality
I'm a donkey's jawbone; create a scar in political metaphors
I'm a silence; shadow hovers over the lunatic world
I'm a noise; fill the ear with the world just as anyone knows it
I'm a drunkard; fill my mind with asclepiadaceous wine
I'm a god; create and recreate myself to have men cast doubts
       on me
I'm a mountain in the dawn; crouch out of the sun before it
       splashes
I'm a truth; run the throat with an alkaloid taste
I'm a lie; the cholesterol of hope grows into a tree and shoots
I'm a dream; always want to be a dream inside closed eyes
I'm a forest; shoot shrubs into the belly of the sky
I'm a whore; embrace the world with the fear of a saint
I'm a saint; the world embraces me with the anxiety of a whore
I'm a priest; Christ tells the world I'm a physician
I'm a follower of Christ; don't need eyes, food and shelter
I'm a follower of the world; need eyes, food and shelter
I'm a sea; five thousand whores rumple my bed every night
I'm a bathroom; print pictures of shame
I'm a bastard; chewed many times like mutton
I'm a road; very conscious of my eyes running into tomorrow
I'm a tenant; owe the landlady a lot of stones
I'm a fire; the undying brother, now, every day and anytime
I'm a cowhide dung; plaster me on outer walls

I'm a temple; hold my body tight, dead or alive

I'm a fighter; food goes nowhere other than in here

I'm a preacher; like my beer chilly cold

I'm a graveyard; long for the smell of the living

I'm a window; spit fumes back at the cobra

I'm a coin; slide into the throat to choke the man

I'm a book; suffer the lunatic mind

I'm a bull; allow many moons to jump over me

I'm a man; ache in the absence of a woman

I'm a pen; pour my ink in composing surreal poetry

I'm a child; suffer the mortal to witness the man

I'm a dog; sick with rabies and of eyes running blood

I'm a death; hate it when they say my hand is cold

I'm a cloud that moves across the sky; no, not really, an amoeba

I'm a fathomless bottom; no, not really, a fathomless top

I'm a clock; no, not really, time, opposed to clocks

I'm a porcupine; no, not really, a super power opposed to war

I'm a fatalist, killing the fratricidal brother; no, not really, clean
　　　the earth

I'm a raindrop; liquid plumages fly right into death traps

I'm a father of four; still to draft my ten commandments for one

I'm a soldier; though no country to defend against any country

I'm a futurologist; store milk in my balls and beers in my penis

I'm a universe; two thousand unknown planets in my wild

I'm a victim; suffer the death of the friend and foe, my own
　　　death too

I'm a slave; I'm running forever on a wild landscape
I'm a smoke; I yearn to be a cloud in the belly of the sky
I'm a poet; Gbanabom Hallowell, bleeding dry

MY IMMIGRANT BLOOD

America
I do not come to you as an exile,
because you yourself are in exile.
I see in your dolorous face the blue
nostalgia to swim the ocean to rediscover yourself.

Why does blood run in your Mississippi? O Masala!
With which leg do I step into your house?
Which hand do I stretch to meet yours?
How do I announce my arrival?

I come reading your palms in university books
and I drink from your Pierian spring
to understand the names of your roads by heart!

I am aware of your two doors that your polished ladies
open up to me, and I come well prepared for your kind
of living water; what baptism
you've got to offer, and with what tongue? America after
meeting you, I see that one does not sketch you from
outside your two doors.
You are like a lizard
that eats a prey whole, passing it through your
thorax, and then your bulbous heart, between lukewarm breasts

I leap in your womb when I think that you are made
of rocks, when I come closer to your sweating skin,
and that part of your body that has grown tired of reasoning
with your hunger, your thirst and your mortality.
All of these make me leap
with the fear of a baby coming
out of her mother's womb and falling into this perfidious world.
I'm scared of your size; I cannot comprehend in my own size.

I'm not quite sure how is it that
I should embrace you in the dawn
and even yet still at the hour of breakfast;
how do I embrace you in the noon when you prepare
for your sophisticated evening rest? I have refused
to ride a bicycle toward your heart where the used moons
of the world begin their lessons of love, even though I too
have brought with me my own ways of showing affection
for a relationship struck under the wet nose of Vermont
where I have crossed paths with your many fine poets.
I have no time yet to buy one of your calling cards
to return voice-cargo to Africa
and remember Ouagadougou
or myself bathing in the Zambezi,
the Kalahari where my lips went dry several times,
the Horne where I tipped the gods daily with prayers.
I have seen your high mountains, but

my heart is still choked by the black rocks of the Kilimanjaro
and sometimes I wonder whether I'm not just its shadow.
I hear the loud groan of the Nile making love to the desert,
and I imagine how she stretches her hand to feel its warmth.

It is interesting America
to know that no one here is familiar with the sun and the moon
I'm familiar with in Africa, and that whiles ours sleep
in our shrine, you actually pluck yours from the sky
and squeeze them in your night beds. And your stars, yes your
stars, I cannot understand why they like to dwell
among you. Ours are too shy to make love in the sky.

America
you are a crowded one; your belly smells
like that of an old lizard. I suffocate easily in your
inside, but that's the beginning
of birth. The new baby always
chokes first when let out in the ocean.
America, you look like the undone face of a rhinoceros.
How come my legs do not hurry out of your
belly where I witness your
children, instead of driving
they are being driven by their cars; instead of eating they
are being fed by their food; instead of working they are being
worked by their jobs; instead of loving they are being loved

by their gods; instead of praying they are being
prayed to by their souls; instead of learning
they are being learned by foreign scholars; instead of knowing
they are being known by others; instead of moving
they are being moved toward; instead of seeing
they are being seen by their shadows.
All I ever hear anyone say is America! America!

Beware, O America!
I come before you singing my sad songs
with drums in my throat and tambourines in my heart.
My skin was gray on my way here,
on my way walking on your silent avenue.
I journeyed between your many flames
which spread in your forests, and I quietly swept my desert feet
through your lugubrious centuries,
scraping a bit of myself with your sharp stones each mile.

I have been told you are a land of two seasons,
a land with the smile of spring and the laughter of summer;
and that winter with its pine needles
autumn, which is also fall, with its deceptive looks
and its itching feet
are prodigals flying over your head with pig's feathers,
inhabiting the earthless land your weeds don't grow.
It is said that these seasons always invade your belly

when you go to bed with your lover
or when you forsake your many gods; so
I scraped my skin, that part of me that has no agony,
that you may embrace me in the seasons you know best.
Being a man of two seasons myself,
I have learned the temperament of the calendar days,
and so though spent, I come before you
in a green mood; a flag of smile;
a heart of innocence embracing you fifty two times
within the bodice of your skylark.

Toward the end of the avenue I turned yellow; but that is the
        color
of a traveller seeking an abode away from a home of war.
Do not fear my looks or the tired clothes draping my body,
nor let my silence speak ill of me,
let not your heart be bothered by my scars;
and although a hurricane is going through my soul
I'd pissed all my malaria
before setting at dawn
tormented only by the common dew
begetting winter here and Harmattan in Africa.
I went through the fjord, the two doors of the sea
before reaching you, America; the Atlantic has two
doors: the sad one and the lost one. I do not know
your sad or your lost door, so halfway through this journey

219

I bestrode your own two doors waiting for your mapquest
to appear on the screen of your eyes of rainbow .

Tell me, America
what figure of speech are you? What animal sound
was it you uttered to me when I scraped my skin
in your bush path? I am tormented
by the long legs of your daughters.

As I grow familiar with your smell and your face, I meet with
many hard objects in my dream; sometimes it's a plain rock
sitting in the middle of nowhere,
other times it's a crouching mountain.
I have also encountered shapeless and undefined objects;
but I come away from all these with a new perception, that
one is not an exile, one becomes!

NATURAL SELECTION

Of the fireflies dancing in my face, the river
is the most sanguine; my black face has no music
so everything comes upon it with the broken
rhythm of temperaments mumbling.

Unless I wink my eyes in rapid succession,
there is always going to be a disagreement
between my gene and the general mind of the gods
regarding the boats sailing in the wastewaters.

I have grown tired of seeing naked beds, tossed
and turned in the middle of a thought only
because a few idle gods sit at the end of the river
feeding the famished oases of a heaven where

the turned-around deserts of mankind take refuge
from a hostile science. This river is the age of my
anger, older than the stone that is by far older
than any god even those born out of necessity.

This moment I cross paths with a god, a lone god
in the waterways; no wonder the waves are arguing
with the wind about the cruelty of death, even on
the gods who are themselves whipped by its rattan.

My eyes are already heavy from squinting trying
to keep up with the boatmen and the boat gods
dipping their paddles into the throat
of tormented river, the sea inside me!

I LOVE THE BREASTS OF WANGARI MAATHAI

... the old janitor on his deathbed
Who demands to see the breasts of his wife
For the one last time
Is the greatest poet who ever lived

"Breasts" by Charles Simic

Nobel, you have finally coughed up my soul
Defining peace in green leaves
Goya you might as well go to hell
With your gothic mind
That has fed me green water paints
All my African days.
The sea inside me has found an environmentalist
And I spring to the sky
One tree at a time until the world
Beholds my medicinal herb.
They knew not the woman
When the ancient Europeans named her *aprica*
Now she opens the old books and writes them anew
One tree at a time
One tree at a time.
The pot which boiled Shaka Zulu's body
Rested its bottom on the breasts of Wangari,
The breasts he kissed before going to war

O Kenya, why did you teach me the lyric?
You didn't write: *In Nairobi there are so many big men*
When Wangari Maathai was marching

Into your forests to find your seed
And when she found it, did she not
Sow it in your belly
Sing with me, Mazrui;
Sing with me, Ngugi;
Sing with me
Nobel, you have finally coughed up my soul
On the bare breasts of Wangari Maathai!

THE BRUTAL DISCOVERY

When God broke my rib and weakened my cave,
I became the extinct. The woman crossed my path
In the Neanderthal morning; that hour the desert stone
Shook off the dust of the beige centuries which had drawn
All its life from the patient magma. She stepped on the eye
Of the globe exactly at the hour the lost centuries were thrown
Out of the Garden of Eden. The stone breathed into my nostrils
the image of the first stallion Adam gave a name to.
I choked in the lungs because of my gluttonous thorax, and The
carcinomatoid apple I received from Adam turned me into a
vagabond tree after tree root after root. I was first the Abel
before I became the Cain, and suicidal of the flesh I shattered
the first mirror I ever saw my image in to put off the Hay
of fire God sent upon the head of my alter-ego. I did not
Know why God consumed sacrifices; and there I was looking
for that one rib I always owned.

DRINKING FROM THE CUP OF LIFE

"The diseases of the soul grow more obscure
as they grow stronger; the sickest man
is least sensible of them."
                    --Michael Montaigne

Seneca, do you want to go at length with me
just because I hauled Spain and ran all your
noisy miles, reading your father before discovering
your beleaguered bones? If I knew your father
it was not so much as the equal of Christ, but
there *you* were many years later studying
philosophy, plucking your orbs to store your miserable
reasoning in your two sockets. O Seneca!

In the end your eyes are not as red as hell.
Better a single room to brood inside than a mansion
where the desert stone rolled off my mother's breasts.
I have an ear for the silent particles of my race, Seneca,
that which you lost to Nero. After today I shall read
you no more because you faked death to be death itself.
You angered the rock, you angered the volcano,
you angered the tornado, you angered the desert.

O Seneca how could you think the infant in your hands
was Christ when you betrayed the exile to the capitalist?

The infant is indeed you missing the jigsaw in your cyclical
journey! I have seen all your sandals in my dreams,
and I know how many steps you took to become a philosopher;
but if the poet does not fear the emperor who fears you,
it is because Vergil offers me a dance in my heart
with one leg raised. For as he puts it, "I know the traces
of the ancient flames." I peg my genealogy on Vergil!
Seneca, you came out of exile leaving behind,
that brother whose only philosophy it is to die for the poor
and not for himself, being that Christ is the two thieves
nailed to the right and to the left, urging the exile to return
and to stay. I am reading you again the next day because
Ovid is making love on the rocks, and because in reading
you, I am wounded, I am wounded by your books! And when
everything else is dead in them, the leaches creep
out of your rotten ink to suck the idle pages.

Okay Seneca, the night is too young to hide in it. Let me
hear you confess what the stones already know, that it was
you who tempted Christ to be suicidal, and you turned around
and envied his tree of good and evil. Seneca, you are not
dead because you are not the one to die. Dying is a gift of
    nature
given to a fortunate few; killing is your duty because you
are a philosopher; and you are awake as a desert stone.

LEGACY OF THE DAMNED

After the guns have been around for so long
I say to myself, mostly over a pint of beer
which is never the last one, that my father's
concubines are heavy on my back. They do not
come upon me with blue erotic hands,
but with the trunks of tigers which become
rattan midway. I feel the pain of a slave
running deep hooks into my skin. O hunter!
leaping into the new century bestriding time,
why elephant? Why not hippopotamus,
why not rhinoceros who only has an ugly face
hunting people with a reptilian stubbornness?

Now I hardly open my window at daybreak
to see the green muscles of God breathing
into my lungs to wash out the beers of last night.
I hardly see the blue shadows of the dead
returning to their graves after a night of labor.
I remember that every other morning, my eyes
caught the images of those little children
born when the earth was flat; my eyes used
to catch their images in the last minutes
the door of the moon was left ajar before the long
hand of lightning twirled around the doorknob
to shut heaven and hell in one big room.

Today my own room gives off a stench I'm not
familiar with, and I live in it as a prisoner, having
locked the door and swallowed the key last night,
running away from the big broad chests of my father's
concubines who crouch in the dark below my stairs
like a new tenant in a graveyard. O, for a place
where my father had never laid a thought! I have
lost my Freetown to the whores, and I must *vanish*
before the man from the sun hunts for the man
of the earth. My country leans its many sorrows against
the grave of its living, since it lost its only child among
oil beans. My only hope is the heartbeats of the dead.

My countrymen are busy jubilating; the morning
has replaced the night, and I'm still here tamed
by a drunk elephant, snorting the last good angels
on the wind. I can hear my people singing, how
treacherous the night was; how deep its memory
of hate. "The night lacerated us and our children!"
they sing. They converted rhymes, "Who has seen
the sun, neither you nor I, but when his rays come
shining by, the night goes fading out!" I take the night
and place it in my heart and think about it. Of the long sip
I had of my beer in the long corridors of Night's four walls, as
I listened then to the long polished legs of time
scraping passed me. I sat inside its thickening

smoke, dressed like a shadow, and I looked deep
into my eyes taking a long sip of my empty bottle of beer!

THE MILLION MAN MACRH

The reptilian man, fixing his lone
tooth to speak the throat,
dragging his memory along the impossible
avenues of Washington, D.C;
the guanaco cutting a sleeve of grass
to seal the age of the yoke, leaned on
the great witness walls
of congress and the capitol;
the behemoth coating
his boils to emerge from the scriptures,
towered the apexes of the American
cathedrals;
the dinosaurian brother
patching his breasts and stepping out of extinction,
leaped over the continental bar.

Each man bringing along an old sun
and an old moon, the stale oceanic
waters and the yesterday
woods of the larvae of pain,
marching the long black streets
with a million desires.

The ruined city on broken tarmac,
these roads of garrisoned flesh,

231

of burnt-out marriages,
of severed tongues and mutilated
umbilical cords, of blood of rain and
of reign of blood, of buckets of tears
alkaloid of proud metals and sweated bodices
of the men marching darker and darker
into this bold territory which once obliterated
their footprints. They carry their "American Dream"
on the banners of their breasts with tormented souls.

Unending chains pulling out of hearts,
coiling around lynching trees O landscape
of the Americans! "Land of the free," where
are your two breasts of memory the sun and
the moon offered you, even when you tortured
God, leaving him hanging black in your winter trees?
O half brothers of the Americas, go back and look at your
old suns to see how many fires razed yesterday
and at your old moons to see how many cities
drowned. For whom does the Atlantic sing her dirges,
those indefatigable waves beating their own breasts
on oceanic banks? For what reason is the sky
catching fire? Soothe this man—
this million man marching!

NIGHT OF MY WRATH

Quedeme a calentar la tinta en que me ahogo
y a escuchar me caverna alternativa,
noches de tacto, dias de abstraccion..

                  --Cesar Vallejo

I do not know how to await the dictator's death
with this deep Bermuda inside me

Others are in the desert
drinking and pissing their blood

Others still are moonwalking their legs
hoping to arrive at the hour the hills kiss the sky

I do not want to travel their road, already
the vultures are too often in that arena

I have gone through layers of ashes, in short
I do not anymore remember how to walk the ordinary wind

My heart is urgent, and the common green
leaves no longer taste of the bitter medicinal herbs

The clock in my breast is too noisy
and I'm tormented by the way it opens its legs to my soul

I'm too organic a man
to avoid the road and walk the bush path

But like the wounded buffalo in the rainforest
I shake off the wet leaves on my back and branch the
narrow path

Licking my blood with a rage
very much like that of the Medusa

The lamps are short of oil in the city
and the streets are closing in on the beggar and the urchin

The avenue becoming the lane
the lane becoming the lonely path

The night has lost its pants
after the beggar cried, O night and after the urchin cried, O
     night

The dictator is in his mansion laughing his sides out
at the joke that the beggar and the urchin fart into the big
black night

And that the miner while coughing blood
farts into the lungs of his disgruntled wife

And that a mad man curses at a mangy dog
who had scavenged and chewed off his rotten toe

We have been in the dark for too long
that no one knows when the rooster will crow

Only the moon could tell where the rooster had flown
to, or whether the sea came to hunt her in the thick of night

A woman down the road is crying,
agony has attacked her breasts and sucked them dry

A whore staggers in a sidewalk because
her pride is pregnant with pain

A grave digger stumbles in the dark
to spy on the grave of the dictator's wife

Whom the dictator had killed to wear on her
his bullion to be banked in his dead god's heaven

I hear a crowd in the night searching for a penny
on the dictator's trail; on that same trail, I search for a
        sword

I hear the invocation of two blind men who search
for the dictator's dining table; I follow after them to strike

O Vallejo, like you I stay on in my cavern
I keep vigil in the night to murder the joy in the dictator

and offer him the agony of the poor; this is my Crusoe
and it is for this I share the cold bed of the night ant

I'm the suppliant hour
urging the metric night into my dawn
And finally when my poem
jumps for the throat of the dictator

With its blade-end iambics, a new hymn shall be sung
for the republic, a new flower shall shoot the sky

And the Bermuda will go to sleep
to allow the rooster to announce the break of day

TOUCH ME EVERY SO OFTEN

Send those blows to fall in the November
boxing ring. I am my own spectator and
entertainer too, that is the madness of exile.
Sweet madness full of boots,
full of the candles of the sun,
and of the edgy shape of the moon.

Let my sore body feel the grips
of the rattan you spanked me with yesterday.
You, this mistress, angered by my teeth
and my notch which keeps
coming to the mouth like a prodigal.

My soles ooze oil no more
because I have arrived where
my feet have pegged the distance;
and I shall grow no more older
or younger—I'm imprisoned!

Life takes a halt!

The calm wind of exile
blows against
my lacerated body,
picking pine needles

237

with the two fingers of a fork.
My mind has a tongue,
sweet for strange lands and strange fruits
so that when I think very hard
with my head, my eyes
are cleared of time blindness.

I'm not the coelacanthine offspring!
I'm rather the phoenix of the stars.
Country, I'm your word, speak to me,
talk me to the wind; fill the belly of my
desert with the wild animals of your hate
and the wild animals of your love.

Seize me by the legs
with the controversial left hand.
You ignited the fire that burnt me, alcoholic!

O exile, doors of my doors!

The green door leading
to the gray door goes into the blue door
and comes out weak; into the mauve door
and comes out sour; into the pink door,
the brother of the half door.

Whenever you feel the sun going the wrong way,
touch me;
the sun lusting after the moon,
touch me;
the stars missing their lenses,
touch me.

Clasp me with your paws,
the stubborn nails on which wild intestines coil.

I SAW THE SKY CATCH FIRE

...the world is different in many places
                    Philip Levine

Ecological degrees are dropping on me, and
I leave my old shoes at the door.

I leave them beside other old shoes
and walk the rest of my journey

on my soles. I merge my spirit with the new ecology.

No one drives a car here, you
sit in it and it takes you

through to the past. A car takes me through a rural path
and hands me over to the sea, the big sea which eats me,
and after which it rages and rages

I sit in the car again, and it takes me
through to another past.
But I soon grow tired of seeing
familiar suns, moons, and stars,
and all the while my body
remains nasty. I soon get tired
of being ignored by the people

I know very well, people who had lived
the lives I see them living again.

A big bird flies over my head, but it
had actually flown by last week,
and has since moved into the future, while
I'm condemned to relive the past.

Imagine that I kill that big bird or the old man now
coming toward me with a crooked walking stick.

Imagine I have a gun and shoot him down,
not a drop of blood would appear, in fact not
even his body will hit the ground because that old man

actually passed by three weeks ago with a cat
cuddled under his arm. That old man
will still be there in the future, just like he is now,
cuddling his cat.

I pass a half dog licking its wounds.
The trees of the long forests on both sides of the road
are grabbing the sky with their branches,
and when I look below them, I see their roots
pulling them to their graves.

When forests grow old, they get trapped in cages.
I can see why they howl every season.
I pass the hills which haunch quietly on their deserts.
I can see every rock, every stone and pebble
under, waiting on the giant brothers.

You have heard it said that
the past is a foreign country, but I tell you,
it is a patina the tomorrow we always feel we don't know:

The familiar brother in the fire, sweating it out,
the dug out grave of the last dictator, the rendition
of the choir of the old cathedral coming through
the high window in a troubled language.

I'M WALKING ON A FINE BRIDGE
ACROSS TO LUNGI

I'm walking on a fine bridge
across to Lungi; I'm walking on a fine bridge
I'm seeing manganese in the water
and I'm seeing the fishes
eating their teeth out on the manganese
and I'm seeing them drinking
the oil that runs into the ocean
and I'm saying to myself, aren't these
manganese and oil resources which the leader
wants to pay for this fine bridge built under my feet?

I'm walking on a fine bridge
from Freetown to Lungi
to entertain myself in the election
promise; to think that I shall die
no more on some rotten UN helicopter
or some Guinean plane piloted
by blind Mandingoes. I'm breezing my hand
on the fat rails running through to Lungi
because I myself have become a flight

I'm walking on a fine bridge
where the Rokel meets with the Atlantic
where the bridge will, at the mere push of a button
open its legs, and ascend the skies

243

like the Christ, and again like the Colossus
bestride the Rokel and the Atlantic
where the Aberdeen creek broke its neck
and petty men like myself in petty
canoes shall pass under
to berth in the comfort of the shore

From the fine bridge across to Lungi
I can see the pregnant wife of a beggar
a woman who is also a beggar, giving birth
to triplets of urchins, and other wives
of beggars who have themselves given
birth to triplets of urchins coming
around to rejoice the births; and I can see
the fathers at the foot of the cotton tree
begging for alms to feed the urchins in the cradle

I'm walking the tarmac of the long
bridge across to Lungi
to see the twin promise of the Bumbuna
to see the magnificence of the night, and
touch the pillars of electricity, the halogen
bulbs, and the solar panels
to see the face of the new city, to witness
that hour the leopard of Tentefor reaches
for the right hand of the lion of Masoila

244

I'm on a mission to Lungi on foot
leaving the ruined city of Freetown
walking on the fine bridge
the leader of the land built
with the diamonds of Kono; I think
about his sleepless architects working
on a number of plans to keep the leader
permanently bridging the gap
between my hunger and my ignorance

I'm on the bridge seeing
the things I had never seen before
in my life: in the water the shrimps
are waving goodbye as they step into Korean
vessels with their Lebanese passports
and Chinese visas; I'm seeing the barracudas
chained and thrown into ancient schooners
as they are taken into slavery; and at the bank
of the river the minas, doomed
to become *bongas*, mourn

How pleasant to walk the fine
bridge across to Lungi! Sad is his lot
who in a life time will never walk the fine
bridge across to Lungi to behold
the uncommon things of the land

I can see the clay walls of Fourah Bay College
which I once thought were pillars of steel
I pause on the bridge to capture
the scene of students going down the slope
but all I see are morose professors
graduating the university

THE PLACE WHERE PEOPLE
DANCE NO MORE

Never mind if my saxophone
is not fingered
in the right spot to open
those bellies that took us
three hundred years to sew
with eyeless needles.

Who wants to play
a saxophone any way
and turn graveyards upside down
for a world full of wedding mismatches?

We play music because it is itself
an ode to Nothingness,
of eyes hanging before
the scarf of the red sun
or that of the gray moon
looking at us
with its two blind minds,
dripping of blood its body
has learned to reject, scarf
either of colors of plain self,
that is, the Nothingness that
it is, that material fact my own
body has itself attempted to reject
in saxophone denials.

But suddenly the scarf
is restless in the wind, beating
threadbare cords, *lap lap lap lap!*
The fool says *everything is music!*

The partially deaf distance misinterprets
the fool, *every tree, every tree*
is, is music, music! But the fate
of distance is like the tragic
laughter of the car-tire on the car-tarmac.

I brand my saxophone against
the flying wind on whose arms the scarf
is already perched with all its tunes
leveled all minors.

Tonight when the lead singer
losens his deep voice to the wind
only the saxophone would fill the air
with its long whistling, breathing into
everything that is Nothingness, and I'll
be sitting in the stillness with a beer in my hand.

OF EXILE AND CERTAIN THINGS

I edge on a stool drinking vodka.
I join the line wasting on the sides
dripping desert rain. Mouthwash,
palm wine of the soft
lips, calabash wasting
on the rocks. Buttocks
grease on grass,
green leaves with yellow skeletons.

I feel the river,
I feel the streaming of the water
in the river. I feel
the flow and the cupped palms
of the receiving end. I drink the vodka
in the glass, and I feel the palm wine
running down my throat. Still sitting
on a stool and listening
to the laughter of the real vodka drinkers
scraping their glasses,
and I, a mahogany man,
pick up my glass quietly
from the fallen body of Pushkin;
and again I feel the taste of palm wine.

Gbanabom Hallowell

My tongue lies. This tongue that tasted
the porridge of my dream last
night. It lies to my body
at the same time licking
the body's sweat; the body sweating
from going around the world
all in one moment,
and resting on a greased
stool offering me two sides of Vodka & Co.
The rain outside drops
but not quite well; the rain inside drops
quite well. I pick my vodka in the rain, a river
runs in the glass. Palm wine foams on my upper lip,
winter frost. *Palm Wine Drinkard*[9] greasing grass,
pick a glass of brimming river, wine, calabash gorged,
city caves in memory lane, lay the ghost in a room for rent.

[9] *Palm Wine Drinkard: Title of a book by Nigerian Writer, Amos Tutuola*

AND OF EXILE AND CERTAIN THINGS

The lane ends this far
and then the path, hoping
it will be the road after the desert
clears the forests. The peninsula
has gone and returned. This is the moon's
new ecology, always been
an old moon with a new ecology. Always been
the exile packing a bag, making
reservations, always been
the tongue
licking the blood in the face,
always been a shadow
on the wall, planning;
always been the rain patting the back.

Always been a beer on the table,
always been a suicidal fucking,
always been rumpled faces
on helpless sheets guilty and starving.

The path ends,
the village opens like a wound;
the sun has been red all day
working, as usual, on the bullion.

The day ends in promise,
pick up the next day
like wind; move the forest
downhill. Will not
be a lane, a road, or a path.

Folded long
before the village budged, that is after
we'd moved
the borders to the bottom of the hill.

And then the night comes with
its casual silence, only to screech where
the forest once was. The moon orders
a sudden stop! The moon
has suffered a heart attack.

All from my room where this time
only my face remains rumpled, no beer
sits on the table, only the packed
bag on the floor, my window sits
on my lap, opening
the larger picture of its mind to me.

AGAIN OF EXILE AND CERTAIN THINGS

In the end I threw all the shadows
out of my room with their bags full
of their grievances. They had come to me
seeking shelter, telling me they were
man-child of the promised land. I knew
I didn't trust the philosophy that invented
them, so we negotiated, and they left their
sandals on the doorway. Who smells of exile
has no ghost, but I was too engulfed in my
own Rwanda to even see the white palm in the black night.

YET OF EXILE AND CERTAIN THINGS

So that many years later when we think of the knives
we also think of the handkerchiefs and of the brothers
who would not stop laughing until they were out of sight;

and of the round table covered with double mackintoshes hiding
under them party shoes carpentered with the funds
of the republic; party men who would talk of seeking re-election
in many ways more than one;

and of the fake death of the fake daughter whose corpse
flies in a Diplomatic Pouch with a belly stuffed with
the diamonds of the hungry countrymen
who are forever applauding speeches delivered in dead tongues;

and of the fowl in the barn that pauses silently with one leg
raised to condemn in its chicken head the actions of the rogue
politicians who beg for votes in public places and in private vote
to share the nation's notes.

It is of these and other things that exile is issuing more passports
than any country in the world; it is of these and many other things
that all the countries have lost their citizens to Crusoe's parlor.
It is of these that the exile shall be an exile!

THE PERMANENCE OF PAIN

I drank every raindrop pouring down on
my country, filling my thirst with living water,
while my peasant countrymen suffered under the yoke

of the country compradors. To this end, I placed
my chances on the rooster's eternally accurate
morning throat to be alerted to this season's

temperament, in case the fallen in the prairie
vomited blood. Everyone wanted the dead
to be buried with the respect they deserved.

I prayed for the helotism of the two eyes of day
which gave me the virgin silver water of fading
clouds. Standing in the middle of the grassland

I could hear the wind shovelling the ghosts
of the dead and my own throat whispering in fear
of the gargoyled household of God, driving unbridled

horses into the night. The barbarians came before
the rain could turn me into a Greek god, which I'd
so badly wanted. That was why I spoke very little
to give my throat an immortal power when
the hour ripened; but then the barbarians came;

even when the old corpses offered them
their empty lives, they must still dig the earth to rape
the fresh seeds inside. I noticed then why corpses don't
like the surface of the earth. Who wants to rot on

a surface where the seasons, lacking a rooster's prompt,
miscalculate the desert temperament, jotting into the red
eyes of the sun? Who wants trees to grow

in the inside of him each time a season escapes
into his eyes to seek solace in the inside?
In all that time instead of talking, I beat my breasts

where the rain I'd been drinking had become incapable
of making my country appear as a metaphor of change before
my eyes. The rain was no longer reigning as the animal

of its promise, and that was why I cleared my throat
to hum to its stagnant waters, to soothe its mane in the space
where my rib had been broken in favor of the sister.

I wanted it be known that I understood the rain's frustration,
but with its head inside my ribcage, I was becoming part
of its own sorrow. It was, therefore, proper to be drunk

on its thunder and to become fearless of the presence
of the barbarians feeding on the last strength
of the seasons. I woke the sunlight on the grass
and whispered a red joke into its ears. It gathered
its fat jaws and chewed the laughter to death
The sun invited me to warm my heart of its living water,

and I took with me all the wet clothes of the corpses
who were shivering in the moon after the barbarians
denied their requests. I entered the sun as

the rooster bled in its throat. It was no longer the clock
hidden in the barn of night nor was the rain
any more the white peacock in the belly of the sky.

I looked at my skin; I could feel my breath on it. I felt
for my throat. It was a drum and its sides full of holes.
I had a voice but it no longer hummed. It carried the sound

of the corpses drenched in the moon. My body was as
naked as theirs, and I too, standing on the surface
of the earth deeply began feeling the permanence of pain.

THE BEATING OF BONES

In memory of my mother who passed away
in Freetown, Sierra Leone, July 18, 2004
while I was in exile

I am the child in the reed-field
candle wax burns coiled threads
in my eyes, and I am broken by
the rainbow that fell
off a tired angel's wings—my mother's.
I am the Harmattan child crying,
and my tears gather in the basin
of exotic rivers. Distance lays its
beige hand on my shoulder.
The wind was on my heels
full of the terracotta shroud. I reached
the cornfields and plucked the corns,
the river filled my bucket to the brim,
the foothill yams sprouted proudly.
That day had no volcano in the teeth
when it smiled to me, and
my feet itched to step on the golden face
of the sun spread across
the distant teosinte.
I laid the yams,
I laid the corns,
and I rested
the bucket.

The tall weeds embraced
my tender body and coiled
around me. When I looked up,
the moon was dangling above
my head and toads were croaking
in marshland jazz:

Whose child this is
with happy footfalls
in the middle passage,
whose child this is
in the teosinte?

Tonight the terracotta wind brings grief
to my heart, and the harvest
of corns, yams, and water no longer
mean a thing to me.
Country,
I weep your decennial indignity that hour
you yourself choked
in your tears the carcinoma of the fratricidal
brother butchering and
laughing and licking the sunshine blood
on the unsheathed machete
under your breasts! O Sierra!
I look toward the Atlantic notorious for strangling

black bodies with venom on thorny shores,
and I remember how I wrestled
with it, angered by the long chain of suffering.

www.ingramcontent.com/pod-product-compliance
Lightning Source LLC
Chambersburg PA
CBHW021047090426
42738CB00006B/223